Throughout our lifetime we are profoundly impacted by a very select group of people. There are a lucky few who know when God is directing them along a particular path. Some choose not to take God's path, while others proceed forward. The lucky ones who go down the path will find His blessings. I was one of the lucky ones, and in my case, God's blessing was Brother Larry Reese.

Brother Larry has made a game-changing impact on my life. He is a Christian mentor and teacher. His impact is even more special now that I know from experience that he works at the direction of the Lord. Brother Larry is a Godly man and I thank God for bringing him into my life. He is uniquely qualified to write a meaningful book on the topic of God as our heavenly Father and how He speaks to His children. Brother Larry is an instrument of God whose special connection is one that I have witnessed and received joyful guidance.

—*Brian Fagan*, *Banker and RAFFA Graduate*

I have experienced firsthand the encouraging and life changing ministry of Brother Larry's discipleship training. Not only has my walk with the Lord been changed, I have seen the tremendous impact Brother Larry's teachings have in all the lives of the students. This impact is demonstrated in their increased intimacy with God as well as the abundant fruit they are bearing in their families, churches, and communities. As a Pastor, I am forever grateful for the difference the discipleship training is making in the lives of people.

—*Jeff Sharp*, *Pastor, Rivers Crossing Community Church*

HOW TO LIVE

Messages FROM MY

BELOVED

LARRY B. REESE

How To Live: Messages From My Beloved
By Larry B. Reese
Copyright © 2013 Larry B. Reese
All rights reserved.

For additional copies, visit:
RAFFA Front Line Ministries
www.raffafrontline.org

Cover Design by Greer Wymond | www.thecreativebird.com
Interior Design by Greer Wymond and Larry B. Reese

Edited by Melissa Shuler

ISBN: 978-0-557-48209-2

Scripture quotations are taken from:
The Amplified Bible, Expanded Edition
Copyright © 1987 by the Zondervan Corporation and the Lockman Foundation.

DEDICATION

I have been so blessed to write this seventh book. My experiences with the students enrolled in my Discipleship School has given me much insight, wisdom, knowledge, joy, and the desire to pursue the Lord all the more intimately. Having seen so many lives changed over the past several years, my heart has fallen all the more deeply in love with Jesus, because I see the validity of what happens when we obey and honor Him. He reveals Himself more clearly to us. I want to dedicate this book to those who have blessed my life, simply by meeting them. It is with great joy that I dedicate this book to all of the RAFFA Discipleship Graduates. You have inspired me greatly to seek the Lord all the more, and to Him, be all the glory for all that He has done and will continue doing.

Larry B. Reese

PURPOSE

It seems like so many years have passed since I first began to really recognize God's voice and actually know that it was our heavenly Father speaking to me. Since that time as I continue growing to know Him and to become more intimately acquainted with Him, I have found that our Father's deepest and most profound desire is to spend time with us—to reveal Himself to us and to show Himself to us that we may know what He is like and communicate with Him from that place. The purpose of the devotional messages in this book is to bring us closer to Him. As you read them, my sincerest desire is that He draws your heart closer to His so that you may know Him in His most desired expression. When reading these messages that I have received personally from the Lord, please bear in mind that what Father spoke to me that He wants to make personal to you as well.

INTRODUCTION

The more I write the more I think about why I write and to whom I am writing. I love the students that I teach. They are a remarkable mirror for me to look into and see the grace of God at work and how He has changed their lives through the reading of books and careful times of discipleship. I am encouraged, delighted, blessed, changed, and sometimes overwhelmed when I see how the Lord is changing the lives of so many young Christians as they enter into the discipleship process that this ministry offers. And as a result of seeing such changes, I have asked them to write certain endorsements for this book because they know the ministry better than anyone. Below is an example of how the Lord has changed a life through RAFFA ministries. Enjoy!

"Know, as you read this book, that you are not alone. I think it's probably pretty basic stuff to tell you that God created us in His image and imparted to us a longing that He has, which is that we have a relationship with Him and with each other. The book you are about to read is fundamentally about those relationships.

'*How To Live: Messages From My Beloved*' is a series of messages in which you are both an observer and a participant. The best word I can come up with is communion—with God, with you, and with me. I have known Brother Larry for some time now and I've been blessed to have spent a lot of time with him. Everything that follows is what I have learned from him, and what I believe you'll take away from '*How To Live: Messages From My Beloved*.' God wants to pursue an intimate relationship with you. God wants you to know who you are. Who you really are. God wants you to see yourself accurately, not as others would name you, nor as you would name yourself, but as He sees you and as He has named you. As you turn the pages, know that God in heaven pursues you with all of His might and glory, wanting to have a relationship with you. Know that your neighbors are looking for the same things you are; love, fellowship, laughter, a shoulder to cry on, and with you. So, turn the pages and enjoy these messages from My Beloved—because My Beloved is your Beloved, too."

John Kaspar, Graduate, RAFFA Discipleship School

Messages FROM MY
BELOVED

AN INTRODUCTION

"In the morning You hear my voice, O Lord; in the morning I prepare [a prayer, a sacrifice] for You and watch and wait [for You to speak to my heart]." PSALM 5:3

"In my distress [when seemingly closed in] I called upon the Lord and cried to my God; He heard my voice out of His temple (heavenly dwelling place), and my cry came before Him into His [very] ears." PSALM 18:6

"Evening and morning and at noon will I utter my complaint and moan and sigh, and He will hear my voice." PSALM 55:17

When we read the Scriptures, we see so much evidence that our Heavenly Father speaks to us and longs to share His heart with us as His children. Too often, however, we believe that the Lord has left us alone to make it on our own in this world, not leaving much evidence, except for the

Bible that He is with us. So, oftentimes, we read the Scriptures, searching desperately for God's will, when the key to finding Him successfully, is to simply desire Him—to want Him—to want Him for Him and not only for what He offers or what we believe that we can get out of Him. Our Heavenly Father wants us to be with Him—to know Him, to understand Him, to be very much aware of His personal plans for our lives, so that our lives are filled with excitement, the kind of excitement that propels us forward with desire into our divine destiny.

I have chosen to write this particular book after many years because it seems to be the right time and it seems the Lord is putting it in my heart to do so. I love talking with and communicating with the Lord. He is of the utmost intelligence, sincerity, truthfulness, genuineness, tenderness, and every other kind word that can be said. Sincerely, I have found a source of life in Him, enjoying His voice, His heart, and His desire to communicate with His people. In these pages, you will find written pieces of how the Lord has spoken to me as well as how He desires to speak and share His heart with His people. If you will carefully read the writings with an open heart and a listening ear, you will also hear the Lord's compelling desire for you to join Him in this beautiful communication. Whatever you may have felt about your ability to hear God or anyone else's ability to hear God, this is an opportunity, I believe, designed by the Holy Spirit to engage you in this moment, to hear Him, recognize Him, and know that He is speaking. He longs to share His heart with us and as you read these pages, please know that His primary reason for communication is because He loves us and wants us to be part of what He is doing currently.

DAY

1

"I WILL SEEK YOU."

"I will bless the Lord at all times; His praise shall continually be in my mouth." PSALM 34:1

I will call on You, my God even in trouble, I will call on Your Name. But at this time, Lord, I am not troubled nor is there anything bothering me of consequence. I simply want to be with You—to talk to You and to listen to Your kind response. Oh, my God, only that I should hear You and to know You more as You reveal Yourself to me—not in what You give me physically, but through the revelation of Yourself. I am hungry for You, my God, so hungry for You. Feed me, if You will, until I am fully satisfied with You. And the Lord spoke to my heart:

"Please know, My dear one, My own dear son, when you call out to Me—when you cry out to Me, I do listen. Never be afraid that I do not hear you. And if I choose not to speak to you, do not

13

be alarmed, for sometime My greatest answer to you—My most appropriate answer to you comes in the form of My silence. Be still...know that I am God. Wait on My timing. Trust My time frame in all you do, and if you do, you will never be afraid. Be careful now not to be afraid, trust My words to you—they will not fail, but will always, always prove without fail to be trustworthy and true. I know that you enjoy listening to Me, My child, and I know how much you want to be with Me—but know this with your whole heart—I am always with you. I will never leave you, nor will I abandon you. But move ahead in your faith with Me, trust Me to lead you into places where you have never been with your faith, where your faith grows in power and you begin to see Me more clearly. I long to show Myself to you in ways that you have not yet seen or known so that you can share what you do see (about Me) with others. I will feed and satisfy you when you are hungry for My food, and it will satisfy you—satisfying the desire that you have in your heart for Me. I am the Lord, and beside Me there is none other. Position yourself, My dear child in faith so that when I do speak or long to share My heart with you, you will know where the place of faith is found."

DAY

2

"SEEK ME...NOT IT."

"Then you will seek Me, inquire for, and require Me [as a vital necessity] and find Me when you search for Me with all your heart." JEREMIAH 29:13

"Jesus answered, If a person [really] loves Me, he will keep My word [obey My teaching]; and My Father will love him, and We will come to him and make Our home (abode, special dwelling place) with him." JOHN 14:23

With my whole heart, I have sought after You. Relentlessly, I have set my face to know You, to understand You and to honor and obey Your heart. My dear Father and God, come to me as You choose and show Your heart to me. Increase my understanding of who You are. Teach me how to bless and honor You in prayer and our time together. I know without any doubt, dear Lord, that You hear me whenever I pray or even think about You. My life is filled with compassion for You.

"My son, as you sit before Me, I will reveal Myself to you. When Moses was in My Presence, he learned a lot more than what he heard. He was enveloped in My Presence; My glory surrounded and influenced him. I, the Lord, (yes, that is Who I am); I am closer to you than the air you breathe, and I will not leave you alone. For as I have told you, even in silence, My Spirit is still at work within you. However, My son, know this and know it with your whole heart; when you seek Me, seek Me for Who I am, dear one, and not for what you can get out of Me.

Many of My people do look for Me, and they look for Me aggressively, only for what they can get out of My hand. I want My people—My very own dear children, to look for Me and for Me alone, and to look with their entire being. And when they look for Me in this manner, I will reveal Myself to them. Yes, I will share Myself with them and they will know Me as Lord, God, and Father. I am not hiding, My son, but My people oftentimes prefer the darkness rather than the light, and I do not dwell in darkness; however, when I do appear—make Myself known, the darkness is dispelled and the place where I make My abode is filled with light. So seek Me, yes, look for Me with your whole heart, and as you do, all that you need and even desire, I will grant it to you.

My son, grow to know Who I am—yes, get to know Who I am with all of your heart, and then the things you fear that are common to all men will disappear. You will find that in this loving relationship we have that I am always with you and that there is no place for tormenting and harassing fears in this love relationship of ours. My son, hear Me now and listen and receive what I am telling you into the deepest parts of your heart, and if you do, you will recognize the truth readily and easily and not be torn between two opinions. Trust Me. Then you will know Me the way that I want to be known, for your trust in Me—your steadfast and certain belief in Me, gives Me, (the Lord) the ability to reveal and share and show Myself to you often and in varying ways. So look for Me, the Lord, and not often to My hand, for when you seek Me alone for Who I am, all that you need will be found in that search."

DON'T GROW WEARY...DO NOT GIVE UP!

"And let us not lose heart and grow weary and faint in acting nobly and doing right, for in due time and at the appointed season we shall reap, if we do not loosen and relax our courage and faint." GALATIANS 6:9

"And as for you, brethren, do not become weary or lose heart in doing right [but continue in well-doing without weakening]."
2 THESSALONIANS 3:13

"**I** have known you for a long time—a very long time," the Lord said to me. "**Before anything else existed and before anything came into view** (as far as you are concerned), I already had a plan, yes, a special plan in mind, that I, the Lord, (Yes, I am the Lord); I had a plan right before My eyes and I said to Myself: 'I will cause these things to happen,' and once I have spoken and said what is in My heart and what My intention is, there is no one who can change the mind and heart of the Lord—unless you are wise, My son, and are able to reason as I reason and as with Moses, who interceded on the behalf of Israel, gave Me reason (a holy reason), in line with My very own heart and plan, that I should not destroy the rebellious Israelites. For I did not bring them out of Egypt to destroy them, but I saw right away (and had known even beforehand that they would not honor Me as they should), even so, Moses had My heart alive within him, having fellowshipped with Me, having embraced Me as his God and Father, he knew Me and recognized Me and knew My personal desire for Israel, so he righteously, (yes, righteously) interceded on behalf of Israel.

My son, do not think too little of yourself, that you have no power with Me, your God and Father. I Am the I Am; I have always been and I will always be, and there is nothing that escapes My searching gaze. I continue to look for those to whom I can reveal Myself—to show Myself as God—to bless and honor that person or the People who choose to obey and honor Me as their God.

I am the Living God, My son, and I will always be alive. Do not forget how I have led you along all these years, how I have held you up when you did not have even physical strength to continue moving in the direction that I was leading you. However, I have kept you safe, guarded you well, and supported and blessed you, and have caused all that you do to be blessed, so that goodness may come out of what you do—even as goodness comes out of all that I do. I Am. Following Me, My son, can sometimes be very difficult, but as surely as I live— as surely as I am Jehovah, I will never abandon you or leave you alone. I will come to you in various ways so that you may know that I am with you and that you are not alone. If anyone chooses to follow Me as you have My dear son, that person will suffer divine sufferings, sufferings that are appropriated to him by Me, the Lord, so that if he endures the tests that come with the sufferings, once he has made it through and come safely to the other side with My help, he will have power that he did not have in the beginning.

Remember this My dear one: Jesus did not look the same going into the grave as He did coming out. I, the Lord, His loving God and Father had changed Him completely, giving Him power (influence) over all of My creation. So don't get too tired and give up when you are assailed and overwhelmed by outward tests and trials that seem to take more than they bring, for the Lord your God is with you—to help you.

Learn the purposes that accompany these tests, trials, and moments of suffering. If you do, My dear son, you will be able to master anything—to overcome it, even as Jesus said that He had overcome them (while alive in bodily form); you, too, have overcome anything, if you walk the way that He walked, walking until you see the victory and victory becomes a visible and defined part of who you are, as far as your ability to see it and know it in your mind.

I want you to use your mind, My son, for I have always wanted My people to think, but not as those who are estranged from Me, the Lord, but those who know their God—I want My people to think as I think—to know Me and to even know what I am doing before I tell them or say anything. Once this type of knowing occurs, My son, you will know My heartbeat and not have to pray as much, for you will know the answer (to what you would have prayed for) even before you pray. So know that I, the Lord; yes, I am the Lord, know that I am faithful and that I will keep My word to you, regardless of what I say. Do not grow weary and give up— but wait, wait patiently on Me and all the things that cause you to fear, doubt, be impatient, be anxious, or to worry—these things will lose their power over you, so that you may know the power of the Lord your God and Father and the power that you have as My son."

DAY

4

"I [the Lord] will instruct you and teach you in the way you should go; I will counsel you with My eye upon you. Be not like the horse or the mule, which lack understanding, which must have their mouths held firm with bit and bridle, or else they will not come with you." PSALM 32:8, 9

"Behold the Lord's eye is upon those who fear Him [who revere and worship Him with awe], who wait for Him and hope in His mercy and loving-kindness." PSALM 33:18

"My son, I want you to remember the days when you were younger, when I began speaking to you. You were very sensitive, genuine, and your love for Me, the Lord, was just beginning to develop. As I revealed Myself to you more and more in everyday living, while showing you what you were to do in life, you began to truly know My love for you and how much I wanted to fellowship with you. I wanted you in My

Presence—to be with Me, to be instructed by Me, to feel Me, and to know that I, the Lord, yes, I, the Lord, I am with you. I gave you instructions that you did not understand until you began to honor them—even though you did not know what the outcome would be. And then you began to desire to simply listen to Me, to know Me, as I revealed Myself to you. I showed Myself to you. It was as if I came out of darkness or a dark place where you had not been able to see Me and made Myself known to you. Ever since that day, My dear son and friend, I have continued to show Myself to you and to reveal My purpose to you for this life with some glimpses of what life is like after this natural life, even living by the power of My Holy Spirit.

I watch you carefully, My son. I have My eye upon you because you are faithful, and I see the way you live and walk, not after the old nature or the flesh—meaning, the nature of man without My Spirit. I do not see you that way any more My son, even though you may sin from time to time. I do not see you as a condemned sinner, but as a saint—holy and acceptable to Me, yes, in My very own sight—but not based upon what you did or will ever do, but based upon the righteous acts of One Man—the Man Jesus Christ—the First-born Son of God—My own dear Son, Who was given so that you and all of those who would believe on and in Him could enjoy fellowship with Me now, yes, in this moment.

My son, I have many wonderful things that I want to do with you. I want to walk alongside you, and if you do not see Me physically with your eyes, do not let that bother or concern you, for the Lord your God—yes, I, Jehovah, I will be with you everywhere and wherever you go. There is nowhere you can go without My knowing it. I, the Lord, I am affectionate toward you, for your faith in

Me—your belief in Me captures My heart and holds My attention, for real and pure and genuine faith, My son, is very hard to find.

Therefore, I the Lord, yes, I am your God—the same One Who spoke to Moses face to face and Who called Abraham My friend. I am the same God Who spoke to all of those who have gone on before you and who obeyed My voice. Listen to Me, My son; consider what I am saying so that you may continue to grow wise and to know the difference (readily) between right and wrong and good and evil because of My indwelling Spirit in you. You do not have to seek out to find the difference between what is wrong or right, I will teach you and show you these things by My indwelling and moving Spirit. I will indeed instruct you, speak to you, and give you insight and words that speak clearly to you so that you may be able to (find) and know My will and be comfortable knowing it.

And My son, (the Lord your God says), if you will follow Me with your whole heart—with all that is in you—all that is alive in you—if you will yield it up to Me, your Father and God, I will bless you constantly and increase all that you have, so that you will have more coming into your abode than going out. I, the Lord, yes, I am with you and I will not fail you in anyway. Trust Me now with your whole heart and believe Me. If you are struggling to believe anything that I tell you, then wait—wait—compose yourself emotionally and stand in the place of faith so that your belief will override your unbelief.

I am the Lord—yes, that is Who I am, and I am with you. I will not fail you in any way. I know that I have spoken to you since your younger years, and now that you are getting older and recognize My voice more clearly, I will not change nor alter this beautiful relationship that we have. If it seems as if My voice has or is changing, My beloved son, it is because you have changed and are now embracing My love and Spirit more readily than you did before. And as you embrace Me, My dear precious son, so shall your love for Me increase and My leading you will be all the more easily done. Whatever you do, dear son, do not be afraid. Do not put your whole trust in anything but Me, the Lord, so that you will not be harmed by those who do not trust or believe Me. Walk with Me, and I, the Lord, yes, I will indeed guide you with My eye upon you."

"WHY I WANT YOU TO OBEY ME AND THE BENEFITS OF DOING SO."

"The person who has My commands and keeps them is the one who [really] loves Me; and whoever [really] loves Me will be loved by My Father, and I [too] will love him and will show (reveal, manifest) Myself to him. [I will let Myself be clearly seen by him and make Myself real to him.]" JOHN 14:21

My Father, as I come before You at this moment, surround me with Your Presence. Let me feel Your love as it permeates my heart. Burn me with Your love—let me feel Your holy fire as it penetrates me inwardly. I so long to hear You, Lord, to know and embrace You. Your voice is as music in my ears and Your words satisfy me. It doesn't really matter to me what You say, Father, simply speak. For I long to hear You. I grow to know more and more about You as I listen to You more. Help me to compose my soul so that I do not listen to my own heart, but that I may hear Your voice clearly.

"You have heard Me say that I want you to obey Me," the Lord said to me. "Sometimes, My son, as you learn how to obey My voice, it may sound to you like I am speaking in the form of a "command" or My voice may come across as hard and even harsh at times. This happens in the beginning because you do not know Me completely or the motives that I have for getting you to obey My words. My son, I do not want you to be an errand boy, someone who simply hears "words" from Me and rushes to do those words or to perform acts. I want you to get to know Me intimately. Sit here and I will give you insight and I will show Myself to you through obedience.

My people do not often understand that My instructions are meant to reveal in a visible way that I am the One speaking to them. But I do not want you to seek Me to simply hear Me share words with you, but I want you to capture My heart and love for My people as I communicate it to you. If you will do this, My son, then you will love listening to Me speak, and I will share things with you that you do not yet know or understand, and in communicating with you, the thing that I have desired for you to do before you came into the world will be made plain to you.

My son, I do not speak in riddles or dark speech with the ones who consider Me and acknowledge and desire Me with their entire heart. I know who wants to spend time with Me. I know who wants to sit with Me to listen to Me even as John did and as Mary did, while sitting at My feet. Do not think of time with Me minimally or passively, for these are times when I build a foundation within your heart by speaking with you and in being silent.

I Myself, (the Lord said to me), will teach you how to recognize Me and to know My heart is in all things and I will give you the wisdom to understand the why, if you pay close attention. As you obey Me, My dear son and friend, you will also grow in love for Me. My affection for you will fill your heart and you will begin to see others in the light of this great affection and love. If you begin to know how much I love and care for you, then you will also know why I have commanded that you should love others even as I reveal My love to you.

My dear son, no man can love the way I love unless he experiences this love of Mine in fellowship with Me, growing to know Who I am and what I desire. In My Presence, My son, My desires are made clear to My children—My sons and daughters, so that they may know what I want in this world. It takes time to begin such a relationship with Me, so be careful to sit quietly, calming yourself, and not being anxious for what you believe you want from Me to make your life better or easier. I, alone, am the One Who created you, and I have a personal hand in your life.

Let Me, the Lord, yes, I am the Lord; Let Me teach you and show you the pathway that I want you to walk into. If you will choose that pathway, I will then assist you with My own personal strength (that is reserved for you), so that you will not fail to accomplish that which is already working in your heart and leading you to do on My behalf. I am the Lord and I will never leave you."

"I have manifested Your Name [I have revealed Your very Self, Your real Self] to the people whom You have given Me out of the world." JOHN 17:6

"My dear son and friend, you were not created to serve yourself or to meet your own needs. I am the Lord, the (your) all Sufficient One. Whatever you need, I will see to it that you get it, as you move along the pathway that I have chosen. I want you to understand, dear one, that the pathway that I have chosen for you is the one you would have taken had (Adam) never sinned and brought about the confusion of Satan—not knowing what the revealed (or continually manifested) will of the Lord is. For you were always intended to have full fellowship with Me, the Lord your God."

"Then why, Father, is it so hard to hear from You at first? Why can't we simply hear You and walk with You once we believe on the Name of Jesus? This remains a mystery."

"My son," the Lord said to me. "A man cannot unlearn what he has lived under his entire life. You have read in the Scriptures where it is said that you must be (transformed) from what you are to what I desire you to be. You must understand with your whole heart, dear one, that man was intended to be (righteous) in every way—in his relationship with Me and in relationship with his fellowman; however, if one is out of order, they both are.

Men cannot walk together in agreement unless they are walking in the (Spirit) of agreement which I, the Lord, have given them—to live in them, to be with them, all the days of their lives here in the earth and in eternity. As a man begins to recognize who he is (as defined) by Me, which means he'll be defined in righteousness as what he was created to do and to be, he then begins to recognize My voice clearly. Not only that, he begins to recognize and sense My ways naturally, as it was intended to be from the beginning.

My son, listen to Me with your whole heart. If you will listen to Me each time I speak with you, you will learn more than what you are actually hearing. Because I am Spirit, dear one, My Spirit, (Myself) influences your human spirit that is now alive to My Spirit, meaning, that you are now able to respond to Me and I am able to respond to you so that you may know Me as I am. If you grow to know Me this way, My son, you will be able to represent Me as I am, able to describe Me, what I am like, My true feelings, emotions, attitude, desires. All that I am, dear one, I will reveal it to you.

Man was created to know many things—many things My son, yet in the fall, his ability to learn things became limited (interrupted) because he now spends a lot of time trying (mostly) in his own strength, trying to discern what is right or wrong, and then, mostly for himself. He has little concern for his fellowman, as I intended.

This is why there is a way that seems right to a man but the end leads him right back to bondage—a life of self and not of God. So that is why, My son, learning to know Me takes time. Do not fear the passing of time or that you are wasting time by spending it with Me. I assure you that you never lose anything by being with Me.

Satan has caused My children to believe that I am keeping something from them, when in reality, I am keeping something (all things) for them—they are hidden only from those who do not have the eyes to see. After you become born again, My son, you have the ability to hear Me, yes, but even a baby has to learn to recognize the voice of his mother. Just as a baby learns day by day and even sorts through the sounds he hears, the colors he sees, and the voices he hears, making distinction between them, so must you learn how to recognize Me. And if you will listen to Me with your whole heart, even if and when you do not understand all things, I will help you to understand. But be careful, My son, for Satan is constantly looking for someone to harm, hurt and even destroy, and the desire to know things is often a major downfall for My children."

DAY

7

"O Lord, You have heard the desire and the longing of the humble and oppressed; You will prepare and strengthen and direct their hearts, You will cause Your ear to hear." PSALM 10:17

"I love You fervently and devotedly, O Lord, my Strength. The Lord is my Rock, my Fortress, and my Deliverer; my God, my keen and firm Strength in Whom I will trust and take refuge, my Shield, and the Horn of my salvation, my High Tower." PSALM 18: 1, 2

"Now I know that the Lord saves His anointed; He will answer him from His holy heaven with the saving strength of His right hand." PSALM 20:6

O my Lord and my great Strength, I will call on You for as long as I live. With my final breath in this life, may it be to praise and honor You for all that You have done for me—how You have honored me, known me, affirmed me, and addressed me by name. Surely, You have set me apart, that I may progressively know Your will and to understand and fulfill it in this life. How I love You, O Lord my God; how I treasure each moment with You because You have listened, heard me, and come to my defense. No wonder the angels cry out to You, saying, "Holy, Holy." I am in awe of You, My God, may my continued prayer be to know You, to recognize You in everyday life and not put faith in my faith or my ability to believe You. For, O Lord, my God, You have caused me to know You, to see inside of Your heart and to want it, need it, desire it, recommend it, and to embrace it. For You, O Lord my God are a Rewarder to those who genuinely seek You out, to those who genuinely want and desire You, You will not hide nor keep Yourself from being visible to them. How I love You, O Lord, as You have treated me with the utmost kindness, and my thoughts constantly turn to You even as Your thoughts turn to me. How good it is that we, Your children, have a God and Father like You—One Who constantly has us in mind.

"My son," the Lord spoke to me. "I hear you and I accept your words, for they are refreshing and uplifting, and words that are true. You are not speaking something that you have heard or read in a book, but the words that you are sharing are true about Me and your relationship with Me, for you have seen Me, the Lord, (Yes, the Lord your God), as I truly am and the way that I want to be seen.

My true son, one after My own heart, continue to lay your entire being on Me—all that you desire—all that you believe you desire, and I will show you the right way. Believe Me with all of your heart when I tell you this: "My plans include you, and all that I am thinking of includes those who genuinely follow and desire Me. Although for a very short time—yes, a very short time you have been in what seems to be a wilderness period, I have observed you and you have not found fault with Me, the Lord, neither in words or how you personally think of Me. I have kept My eyes upon you and I see that your heart is pure toward Me, and you have (yet again) passed the testing of your faith. I require you to be a man of power, authority, strength, grace, and one who knows the Lord and is able to describe Me as I am. Surely, you have walked with Me and I have shown My nature to you as you have laid down your own life and chosen the life that I chose for you before you were born. I am the Lord and beside Me there is no other God—Jehovah, that is Who I am, and My Name is written upon you, setting you apart, causing you to be distinguished in My very own eyes.

Do not be afraid, My beloved son, for as you continue to stretch your eyes toward Me, seeking Me as you would daily food and water, I will reveal Myself—showing you in detail, yes, intimate detail, Who I am and who you are. Do not be afraid, I say to you, do not be afraid if it seems you are losing the things that you have in this world, for all that I require of you, I, the Lord, will return it multiplied, just as you have seen in the past. For if you do not allow the things of this world—including what you desire the most and even things I have personally promised you to control you, you will receive them in due time. I will not keep anything good from you. I am the Lord."

"Lean on, trust in, and be confident in the Lord with all your heart and mind and do not rely on your own insight or under-standing. In all your ways know, recognize, and acknowledge Him, and He will direct and make straight and plain your paths." PROVERBS 3:5, 6

DAY

8

"For though the Lord is high, yet has He respect to the lowly [bringing them into fellowship with Him]; but the proud and haughty He knows and recognizes [only] at a distance. Though I walk in the midst of trouble, You will revive me; You will stretch forth Your hand against the wrath of my enemies, and Your right hand will save me. The Lord will perfect that which concerns me; Your mercy and loving-kindness, O Lord, endure forever— forsake not the words of Your own hands." PSALM 138:6, 7, 8

"My son, know with all your heart that I am with you— close to you, listening to you, wanting to be with you, hearing you, walking with and working with you and causing you to know Me, the Lord, more intimately. Although you know Me as being the Lord Who is in heaven, I am also near you—very close to you, to show Myself to you and reveal Myself to you—up-close and personal. I have always known what you would do, even before you were born, I, the Lord, (yes, I am the Lord); I knew what you would do before you came forth from your mother's womb. And I have saved you, literally brought you to Myself based upon what I knew—yes, My foreknowledge of all things has caused Me, the Lord, to bring you to Myself so that I may teach you all things—even the things that you are called to do in the world with My assistance. My son, dear son, I am already aware that you know in your heart that without Me you cannot do anything. You know this well, and yet this knowledge has not caused you to feel inadequate in anyway. My son, tell Me why this does not make you feel inadequate.

"Because I know that Your assistance, My Lord, governs and guides me. You protect me and lead me the right way. I do not look at my inability in following you as a hindrance, my Father, but as a blessing. It causes me to know where my strength truly is."

"Well said, My beloved one. You are wise, My son, and I am pleased with your ability to know the truth. I ask you questions, My dear one, not because I do not know what you will say, but so that in your conversations with Me, the Lord, you will better know the truth in your heart and how to "say" it. You know that I am the Lord and that I only speak the truth. Having been with Me, My son, you are beginning to recognize (naturally) or by nature, what you should have known all along, and this is good in My sight.

So I say to you My beloved one, do not fear, do not become anxious, and do not allow what seems to be the passing of time and days to distract you from what I have put you in the earth to do. But wait on Me, the Lord, yes, wait and be patient, for I will, in due time, perfect (bring to fruition), all that I have told you, and you will see it with your own eyes. My primary concern at this point in our communicating together is to assure you of My Presence, and that

I am forever with you, never to leave or abandon you. Be careful, though, My beloved child to listen to and for Me. Desire My mind and My knowledge and have the constant willingness to obey. If you maintain these godly attributes, you will go very far with Me, and I will speak clearly to you, based upon relationship and intimacy, and you will hear Me. You will then move forth from where you are to where I want you to be and you will see the salvation or the intended purpose that I have for you—constantly before you.

Don't get tired of being patient and waiting on Me; for if you continue to accept what the passing of time brings to you in waiting, you will become as patient as I am. I am patient, My son, because I know what is going to happen. And if you are silent, still, and quiet before Me, you, too, will grow as patient as I am, for My nature, (yes, the nature of the Lord your God) will permeate and burn you like a branding iron, and you will walk in My inherited nature as it was intended from the beginning."

DAY

9

WALK WITH ME

"And out of the ground the Lord God formed every [wild] beast and living creature of the field and every bird of the air and brought them to Adam to see what he would call them; and whatever Adam called every living creature, that was its name."
GENESIS 2:19

"**M**y son, walk with Me," the Lord said to me. And as He held out His hand, I reached for His and suddenly my hand looked very small in His and I became very small, almost like a child, but well kept safe as I walked alongside Him.

"**For a long time, I have walked with you and I have been showing Myself to you in bits and pieces, giving you revelation about Myself. Why are you not afraid of Me, My son,**" the Lord asked. Then for a moment as I continued to walk with Him (in the spirit), I looked into His eyes that were no longer hidden by the fears I once had.

"I am not afraid any more, Father, because I realize I do not have to be afraid." Then He smiled and looked ahead of us as we continued, but my eyes never left His face. **"So you are not afraid, why?"** He asked, waiting yet again for me to share my heart with Him.

"Because I'm beginning to know You better, Father. My heart is no longer fearful but at rest. I have no fear in my heart when I am with You. I used to because I did not know You. You are great, Lord, and Your magnificence intimidated me, although now I wish it had not."

"So then, you are comfortable with Me."

"Yes, Father, I am comforted by You, and by being with You. It seems that everything that could possibly harm me loses its power when I am with You, and that is why I love being with You. I love and appreciate You, Father. Where are we going?" I looked ahead of me and waited for His answer. As we continued to walk, the Lord put His arm around my shoulder and as I felt the warmth of His touch I knew that everything was alright, yet wondered what He would say to me.

"My dear son, things are about to change in your life—not for the bad, but for the good. I always enjoy being involved with My creation, and especially man, so that he and I can work together. That was My intended purpose. I'm walking with you just like I walked with Adam and gave him things to do. Adam was not My slave, dear one; he was My son, and so are you. You are very interesting to Me," the Lord said, catching me off guard with His words. Me? Interesting to the Lord.

"Interesting," I said to the Father. "Me? How?" He smiled and continued moving slowly ahead, His arm never leaving my shoulder.

"Interesting," He said, "because you have faith in Me. You trust Me. My son, let Me compare you to Abraham and even Job, those men in the Bible who are often esteemed for what they did. You are My son and I am well pleased with you. Your faith brings Me out in the open, giving Me the ability I desire to fellowship and have fun and interact with My sons. I want to be with you. I want to reveal Myself to you and share My plans with you. Faith brings Me out into the open—into open view so that I may reveal Myself to those who genuinely seek for Me, to those who genuinely want to know Me as I am. Faith in Me does not make Me Who I am; it does reveal Who I am to those who belong to Me. Your faith makes you whole, dear one; your faith gives you the ability to require and inquire of Me so that I may speak the truth into your heart and your mind is changed. I love being with you, My son, and never think otherwise.

Obedience brings Me out into view, and disobedience hides My face. So be careful to practice being wise when you do not understand My way of doing things. Do not act as if you know all things, when without My intervention you cannot know anything. I will give you wisdom and make you intellectual beyond your years, if you will continue to listen to Me.

I am here with you now My son for a while in fellowship to share My heart with you as well as My desire for you and the dreams that are before Me for you. I am the Creator, My son, and yes, I do dream (as a man) and as God. I have dreams and plans for you that will bless and encourage you, giving you (advanced) vision so that you will occupy and keep busy until I either (come) or require you to do other things. As long as you engage yourself with My activity, you will experience joy, bliss, fun, excitement, growing zeal and delight, and an intimacy with Me that gives Me the ability to speak plainly to you so that you will not need to try to know Me through your memory of Scripture. You have gone through a lot, My dear son, and I have not taken your pain lightly. Even though you have gone through a lot, you have learned a lot and your mind has been trained by the pain you went through to better discern and recognize when and how I am at work. This kind of discernment, My son, is growing and becoming more powerful and practical, so that you may be able to better assist those who are in My church.

You are a gift to the church, My son, called out (elected) by Me as a prophet. You are not better than your brothers, My son, you simply have a gift that I have given you, an ability that has come with years of suffering, and sometimes you felt as if the suffering would not end. I am the Lord, My son, and just as I came to John on the Island of Patmos, I am here with you (in the spirit), revealing to you what My plans are for you.

Listen to Me carefully, you are about to enter into a deep place of intercession, though this kind of intercession is not only in and for prayer as you know it, but it also means that you will stand in the gap and intervene for many by My command. I will put within you the ability to know when this is to be done. Not only are you (sent) to speak My words, but that in speaking them where there has been chaos or disorder, peace can be restored, if those to whom I send you will listen. Surely, I have called you a peacemaker and given you the means by which this peace can be established—not in the world, but within the walls of My own community—My Church, dear one. Your love for Me, dear son, has brought you to this place—again, not that you loved Me, but that I loved you first (from the beginning), and now this love that I have for you has captured your heart and now contains it. I am the Lord. I will govern your life for the rest of your days and I will cause you (instant) blessing. I, the Lord, will recover all that you have lost in every area of your life, because you have walked with Me and have not found fault in My treatment of you. I will cause you to rise up further and further in My power, giving you territory that once belonged to those who obeyed and honored Me at one time, but pride has caused them to fail.

Remember this, dear son, you cannot do anything on your own, and what you have, always remember that it has come from My hands. Save these things that you are writing down and include them in your book, for others will come behind you along this same trail, and I will use this book, this message written in it to encourage those who must walk this similar path. I also understand, My son that you have sometimes felt that your life was given away and nothing would return to you. However, the Lord your God is not a thief nor someone Who takes away and does not return. Whatever I borrow or use, My son, as indicated in the Scriptures, I always return with blessing upon the one who gave.

You are My son and I am well pleased with you—having been in hiding (or unseen) as far as who you are in My kingdom; by Myself, I am now readying you for public view. Surely, you have been on the potter's wheel, and while not always patient, you have surrendered to the hand of the Potter, and I am about finished with you and readying to put you on display. Surely, you will have men contacting and calling you when they find out about who I am creating you to be. And you will go to some, My son, as one sent by Me, and My words—the words of the Lord your God will burn within your heart to speak to them; and these in this hour, My son, will listen to you and receive you. For I am causing My people, those who are truly My own sheep to recognize Who I am and what I am doing, so if they recognize what I am doing, they will also recognize you, the one being sent by Me, the Lord.

For this is the hour where judgment is beginning at the front steps, yes, the door steps of My own church, and yet My own people are asleep, many of them would never recognize a move of Mine because they have been asleep too long, and will find this forthcoming move of Mine disturbing. It will not allow the lukewarm, the careless, the apathetic, and non-perceiving to be comfortable in My Presence. For the voices of the prophets and the apostles—true apostles and true prophets are beginning to rise in My church—My true home, and they will set things in order for this coming harvest of souls. And those many thought were saved will backslide and what is truly in their hearts shall be seen and made known publicly. You have the 'goods', My son, and I am with you. I will protect you Myself, for the prophets are close to Me and dear to My heart, especially those who have been sent by Me with an ongoing and consistent message. No harm will come to those, for they are being held for such a time as this, where the world's economy and everything that men hold dear is beginning to fail them.

Yet in all of this, will men call out to Me, to seek Me, to know Me, or will they curse the One they have never known? For those who have ears and eyes to see will know that I, the Lord, am at work, and I will cause the wealth of the wicked, the unworthy, to be handed over to those who do the will of the Lord, and they shall have no lack. I will do this and it shall be a supernatural work that will not happen to just anyone simply because they call My Name, but it will happen to those who have been selected by Me to do My will who must have the resources to do so. Liken it, if you will, to the day when Israel left the land of Egypt, and the Egyptians gave their wealth to the Israelites. It was I, the Lord Who inspired this. So now, My son, hear Me well as I end this time with you, you are about to cross over into an altogether new dimension of power and wealth so that you may be able to get My work done as I intend it to be done—you will be given all you need to do what I have put you in this world to do. Up until this point you have struggled, or so it may seem to you, to get what you have needed, but the Lord your God has always been with you."

10

"I call to You because I know that You will hear me." And the Lord said to me: "I know that many of My people are distressed and torn within because of all the things they see around them in this world and how it is affecting them personally. However, I, the Lord, do not change. "I Am" the Sufficiency for My people, and these times are demanding an answer from those who say they belong to Me, the Lord. For I asked My (very own) disciples, 'Who do you say that I am?' The times that My people have entered into, times that demand that they know Who I am are upon them—can you say that you know Me as the Lord God, as Jesus the Christ, or are you still trying to find a loop hole out of your circumstances that seem to grow worse?

For I, the Lord, (Yes, I am the Lord), am causing My very own people, My personal sheep to turn and even to return to Me, so that I will reveal Myself to them as they genuinely seek Me and look for My face—until I, the Lord, (Yes, I, the Lord) come out into plain view so that those who genuinely seek Me for Who I am will see Me as I am. I am not hiding, (the Lord says), but as My people, those who are genuinely called by My Name will earnestly seek Me with all of their hearts (with no tendency to have a backup plan), I will show Myself clearly, establish them more certainly in a personal and powerfully engaging relationship with Me, so that what is happening in this world will no longer tear them and pull them away from Me, causing them to have varying opinions of Who I am.

Do you know Me as Peter did, when he clearly said: 'You are the Christ, the Son of the living God?' And I clearly remain, God. There is none other beside Me, and as you seek Me—really and genuinely seek Me with your whole and entire heart, desiring (speaking) truth in your inward parts; then I, the Lord, (Yes, I, the Lord) will reveal to you just what Peter (saw), not by human learning or observation, but by the power of My indwelling, operative Spirit, (already) living in you, Who is alive and desiring to reveal Himself and My true nature to those who claim My Name."

"...My soul, wait only upon God and silently submit to Him; for my hope and expectation are from Him." PSALM 62:5

"...In the morning You hear my voice, O Lord; in the morning I prepare [a prayer, a sacrifice] for You and watch and wait [for You to speak to my heart]." PSALM 5:3

"...In my distress [when seemingly closed in] I called upon the Lord and cried to my God; He heard my voice out of His temple (heavenly dwelling place), and my cry came before Him, into His [very] ears." PSALM 18:6

Father, I position myself to hear You...to listen to You. I calmly kneel here, waiting on You to speak to me. I know that if You will speak to me, dear Lord, the worry and fear and uncertainty that I have will ease. For I know that if You will speak to me, whether You choose to address what I am concerned about or not, I know that You will have heard me. I come in confidence, dear Father, based upon the certainty of Your words to me, knowing that You listen, knowing that You hear, and knowing that You will answer me. I will not doubt my God's ability to speak to me and to set the record straight, whether that be in my own heart, or to give me insight into what I do not know.

Do listen, dear Father, my Friend (as you have called me), and give me wisdom, delight, and joy, in knowing that you have listened to me and kindly shown regards toward my petition. I have no other God but you, dear Father, no other idol or thing has my affection— I long to be with you all the day long, and as a result (of my setting my priorities) in order, there is nothing that hides Your face or the feeling of Your will from me. Father, my soul is disquieted within me and I sense nowhere to put my feet at this time; listen and hear me, dear Jehovah, (my Father), and tell me, where are You taking me?

"...The earnest (heartfelt, continued) prayer of a righteous man makes tremendous power available [dynamic in its working]."
JAMES 5:16B

My son," the Lord spoke to me. "Know (without doubting) that I hear you—that I listen to you when you call to Me. I hear you (each and every time) and without fail. My eyes are upon you—waiting and listening to and for your voice, for you have been trained (by Me) personally, yes, by Me, (the Lord), personally, to speak out of your spirit, rather than out of your fears. For as you call out to Me, (deliberately) and in truth, you can be certain that I will hear and that I will answer you, and that I will set your thoughts into action, giving you the ability to move from one place to another, having received wisdom from listening to Me.

Now, I will listen to you, dear son, but you must also listen to Me. For what makes a man's prayer powerful is not just his faithfulness and belief in his prayer or My ability to answer it alone—but it is also in his ability to (hear back), to receive back from Me that which I choose to speak. For I will respond to you in righteousness, satisfying the righteous desire within you, My own child.

Hear Me, for I am Jehovah—the First and the Last—the Beginning and the Ending—the Alpha and the Omega—the One Who has always been alive, and I continue to live as I am. You have found it difficult to find a "footing" because you are growing to be more knowledgeable of Who I am. I am (raising) your spirit upward and revealing Myself more clearly to you. And as this happens, dear one, it causes inner conflict within your soul. But do not let this bother you, dear son, for I, the Lord am teaching you what it means (by definition) to be in the world but not to be controlled by it.

I understand, dear son, that this can be a bit confusing for you—even causing you to feel alienated and estranged from your friends and family, but it is My will that you should know Me more intimately and clearly. As you continue to yield to Me, you will find that the fear of not knowing where you are or where you're going will disappear. Although this has been a trying time for you, dear son, you are reaching out and calling out to Me more genuinely, purely, and of necessity.

For I am the (Way), I am the Truth, and I am the Life Giver. I will make Myself plain to you in every avenue of life, teaching you how to think (soberly) and clearly at all times. For do not allow this temporary place of not understanding fully what I am doing in your life to cause you to stumble or fear, only continue to seek Me out—just as you are doing now—and I will continue to answer you. I will not fail to lead you in paths of righteousness, which establish My Name in you and in those who believe the testimony that is (developing) in your life. For although it may seem strange, this walk that I have you on, I assure you it will lead to greater power, understanding, and a clearer ability to reveal Who I am to others. Not all men are called to do what you do, dear one, but if you will listen to Me, (Yes, listen to Me, the Lord) with all of your heart, then I will keep your mind at ease and in peace."

And then as I accepted His words to me, I began to feel peace. Sometimes as we walk the pathway that God has chosen for us, it seems lonely, as if no one else is walking along this same path. We can be assured that God knows the way that He has chosen for us and that He will lead us directly and clearly, until we become so acquainted with Him and His way of doing things, that we welcome His ways, and begin to live them out; for God desires us to walk as He walks.

"...For I have kept the ways of the Lord and have not wickedly departed from my God." PSALM 18:21

"...As for God, His way is perfect! The word of the Lord is tested and tried; He is a shield to all those who take refuge and put their trust in Him." PSALM 18:30

"...Show me Your ways, O Lord; teach me Your paths." PSALM 25:4

"...The steps of a [good] man are directed and established by the Lord when He delights in his way [and He busies Himself with his every step]." PSALM 37:23

*"Before I formed you in the womb I knew and approved of you
[as My chosen instrument], and before you were born I separated
and set you apart, consecrating you; [and] I appointed you as a
prophet to the nations." JEREMIAH 1:5*

I said to the Lord, "What is it that You want from me the most?
Tell me, what is it that You want from me the most?" And He
said to me:

"I want you to know who you are. I want you to know who you
are as how I have described who you are and not what you think you
are or how man might categorize you. I am the Lord, and before you
were born, I discussed this matter with your mother, telling her that
when you were (old enough), I would make it known to you who you
are in My kingdom—as you are called, not as what men might call
you. For surely, I, the Lord, have called some men to be pastors, dear
son, but you are a prophet. I chose you to be a prophet.

This is not something you decided to be or asked to be. For
even if you had asked to be a prophet, My son, should I, the Lord,

have obliged you? For in all honesty, you would have not known what you were asking for. For men who ask for "callings" never really know what they are asking for. Do you not know, My son that a true call is to give up all that you know or even hope to be and follow after Me, the Lord? It is a lifestyle that begins (even) before the actual call has been made known to you in your mind. I am God—I am Spirit, and I look for those who worship Me in spirit and in truth. My Name is Holy. It is separated from anything man made, My son, yet I choose to live with, to make My abode with My people—those who know Me by Name.

It is not enough, My dear son that men say they are Christians, but it is well pleasing in My eyes that they know Who I am personally. Am I a stranger? Surely not. I have been around for always, and am most willing to reveal Myself—to share My heart with those who really want to know Me. When I reach out to My people, My son, seldom are they ready for what I am about to do because they are already busy doing what they feel they need to do. If a man does not know that I am able to live with and to abide in his heart, as soon as he stops feeling My Presence, or cannot sense something in his own natural self, he will soon go back to where he was. Faith loses its power in his life for he has chosen to go back to natural living. However, to the man who continues to search for Me, long after I have seemingly disappeared or returned to the invisible realm, I will make Myself known to him. Without operative faith, My son, it is impossible to please Me. I am hidden although I am in plain view, if a person does not use his faith, he cannot see nor find Me.

You ask Me, dear son, what is it that I want from you? I want your devotion and your love, and even though I may speak these terms to you and you have an idea of what they mean, you cannot accomplish them in your own strength or power. Only I can give you the ability to know and desire Me this way. You must will yourself to be willing, and then I will teach you how to do what is in your heart—for desire alone is not enough, for many of My people desire, but never get into the place of doing. Once I have made My desires known to you, My son, position yourself (inwardly) within your heart and purpose to do as I have said.

Although you will struggle to maintain this new position of getting to know Me, I will lead you clearly and sustain you gracefully when you have difficulty. I am the Lord. I want you to know who you are as I am defining you and bringing into light who you were called to be before you were born. Many of My people (including) those who are the most educated, do not believe and would argue with you that I have prophets this day in My Church. You must understand, dear one that whatever or whenever a man cannot explain what he says he believes, there is always room for error and doubt. Man and even Satan uses this doubt against him. Either I have called you to be a prophet, apostle, evangelist, pastor, or teacher, or I have not. You must know these things in your heart. There are some things that man cannot "confirm" to you. Only I can confirm and affirm My call in your life, especially when men fight and argue about the existence of what they consider modern day prophets. The question to them is this: 'Do I, the Lord, change? Absolutely not. Do My people get to the place where they become more dependent upon their knowledge of Me rather than the revelation that I give them from the Scriptures that they read? When men get to the point where they depend more on their learning and mere natural knowledge without any representative power from Me, it is then that I will raise up a stronger voice among them. This voice is known as the prophet or the voice crying out in what has become a place of wilderness, desolation, and progressively estranged from My Spirit, saying, thus: "Repent. Return to the Lord." Many men who have gotten away from Me, My son, never really know this in their hearts, for in their minds they are deceived into thinking that their intelligence and education makes them holy, when in truth, all they have is knowledge without revelation of that knowledge or even to know how to understand it.

You, My son, even though you do not have the education (concerning) Me from the schools of men, you have been with Me, listening to Me in a place where all those who are called can enjoy, but this place with Me is a struggle to get into and to remain within. For My very Spirit will deal with a man, changing him, causing him to see his worth—his true value from a holy perspective, causing him to become nothing until he realizes that it is in this nothingness that I am revealed and he then knows from Me, the Lord, who he truly is. That is why, My son, you cannot rely on the education and systems of men to tell you who you are. Although you may not feel it and see no sign of My Presence or being with you, I assure you that I am. This way, your walking without feeling, you will come to know Me by faith—the invisible God made visible through faith, and when it is time to speak, you will speak, and when you speak, those who have no power with Me and who are only led by their knowledge of Me, which has made them prideful and arrogant, they will recognize that there is a difference in those who speak and who are sent by Me. I have not known these men, My son, nor do they call out to Me to help them to spread My Gospel, but rather, for Me to help them do what they feel is needed.

I am not looking for those who are converted to the gospel message of men, but for those who are converted by the power of the Gospel according to My Holy Spirit, and further discipled into this message and its power. These are the men whom I can trust and reveal Myself to, My son; however, these men are hard to find in the earth. But with this said, I am calling and gathering a new generation of men and women who will honor Me and obey Me and will not care for their lives or themselves. Their testimony will be as Mine—the testimony that they have received through the blood of Jesus Christ, and they shall come forth in power, not loving and clinging to their lives, but their lives are hidden and invested in the Christ.

So My son, listen carefully to Me, the Lord your God, and do not think that you can bring definition to who you are called to be through Bible study—although nothing is wrong with this, but know in your heart of hearts that you have been with Jesus—actually been in His and My Presence, gaining insight and wisdom and understanding into the true nature of the Lord your God, so that you may be able to pass this on to those whom I am sending you to."

DAY

12

"I delight to do Your will, O my God; yes, Your law is within my heart." PSALM 40:8

"This morning when you woke up," the Lord said to me, "And began to think about Me, to worship Me, I began to put My words into your heart and mind. My son, do not forget that I am constantly with you and as you spend time with Me, opening your entire heart to Me, My wisdom and words will find their way into the inner most parts of your being. You do delight in Me, My son, and My desire is to show you more and more of Myself—to reveal Myself to you the way that I really and truly am. I am drawn to you. Because you desire Me, the Lord, above anything and everything else in your life, it gives Me the ability to make Myself plain and known to you in ways that I desire to show and share Myself with My other children.

My son, do not be afraid to express this love that I am putting in your heart. For your life has been filled with many years of pain, sorrow, and disappointment, just as I told you this morning; but I am removing those times from your life physically, and going back in time with you, My son, so that I may remove every debilitating trace of hurt, sorrow, pain, disappointment, rejection and other hurts that were sustained from the unloving. My son, do not be afraid, for as surely as I live, I will cause you to forget all those years of pain. See, before you, yes, before you I am opening up a brand new day and a brand new and fresh way that will bring you great excitement, with a life that is filled with purpose, delight, and pleasure. I will cause you to remember the earlier days no more and you will ultimately be consumed with My purpose. I know that you enjoy being with Me, My son, but pay close attention to what I am telling you. For I, the Lord have purposely pulled you out of where you are, setting your feet upon a firm and strong foundation so that you will know how to walk, where to walk, and to know why you are walking a certain way. It will be just as I have told you, for the Lord says, I will put My words in your mouth. I will be your (visible) God, causing you, My son, to be My voice and mouthpiece. I will send you forward. For you were born to worship Me in this—to speak My words and to share them with whomever I send you to.

For it will be as I have said, I will cause My word to come out of your mouth to revive the hopeless, to cause the depressed to sing and have joy again, to give hope to those who have lost hope—for you are My chosen vessel, My son, My prophet, My joy and delight rests upon you. So go now, My son, and do not fear what you have feared in the past, where I, the Lord, (yes, it was I), the Lord, Who caused you to be given away even to the unrighteous, those who do not love or hold the Lord your God affectionately, but they are also in need of salvation. Fear not and do not worry, for not one day of yours in this earth has been wasted."

DAY

13

"I [the Lord] will instruct you and teach you in the way you should go; I will counsel you with My eye upon you." PSALM 32:8

"I have been watching you My son," the Lord said to me. "I have been listening to your thoughts and examining them. Tell Me what is in your heart My son, and do not hide it from Me. Do not be afraid to tell Me clearly what is in your heart and mind. If you will speak carefully to Me, then I, the Lord your God and Father will put My thoughts in your heart by sharing them with you. I do not want you to live in fear of the future or to make plans around what you are afraid of, rather, I want you to make plans with Me walking right alongside you, so that you can be sure that those plans will be carried out. Remember this My son:

"[Not in your own strength] for it is God Who is all the while effectually at work in you [energizing and creating in you the power and desire], both to will and to work for His good pleasure and satisfaction and delight." PHILIPPIANS 2:13

"I know that it is in your heart to please Me, and I know that I am the first Person on your mind each day. I am ever in your thoughts, My son. Tell Me what it is you feel—express your full heart to Me and I will express My full heart to you. Let there be no secrets between the two of us. Share your heart with Me that I may share Mine with you. For I am a (talker)," the Lord said to me, "A divine Communicator, and I want you to know what I am carrying out. Look," He said to me. "I can see that there are many thoughts floating around in your mind, yet you are not able to put them into perspective, but you do know that these thoughts of yours have come from My influence, do you not?"

"Yes, Father, I know that they have come from You. I think that the most difficult thing is knowing how am I supposed to do what is in my heart to do. You know that I want to obey You with everything in me, and in fact, my every thought centers around You. How can I carry out such beautiful and extensive plans, Father?"

"My son, look to Me continually. Because it is in your heart to obey Me and to carry out My plans, as I show them to you. You must know that I know everything all at once, and I am not holding this over your head to taunt you, but to teach you how I do things and to share what I know with you. It is within your capacity to carry out what I show you. Don't worry or be concerned, you will be able to do what I am showing you. My son, part of your problem is that you have lived so long with an independent nature. You take things upon yourself, once you believe you know how to do them and you try to carry them out. But without Me giving you the ability to do what I show you, you cannot carry out the plans. I do not want you to have the mentality or the mindset of a slave, someone who has no will. You are My son—not just any son, but you are My own faithful son, and My love for you (reveals) and shows you what I am doing and is always ready to direct you. I gave Adam work to do as well as Jesus His work to do. I also gave John the Baptist His work to do, and I continue to do work and reveal Myself to those who obey Me even in this day. My work within itself is finished My son. I am completely sufficient within Myself, yet I have work and plans for you to carry out. These works and plans are within Myself, and the obedient son draws those works out of Me by faith. Without operating in faith, it is impossible to please Me. Without operating in faith that brings about My Presence and power, it is impossible for you to feel My pleasure. I love you dearly and that is one of the reasons that I want to show Myself to you and reveal to you who you are more and more while you are in the earth.

"So I should learn to share my heart more and more with You."

"Yes, My son, you should. For My plans alone will overwhelm you in your mind because your mind (as it is) is not capable of comprehending My greatness or how I want to get things done; however, as you yield what I give you back to Myself, I will make My plans plain to you and you will know how to get these things done. Jesus always knew where to get what He needed. My Holy Spirit revealed (or showed) Him where those things were. Am I any less capable to show you the same things, if you honor and obey Me persistently? I do not want you to be someone who simply runs errands for Me, as I've told you before, I want to work alongside you—to see your expressions when you see how I reveal Myself.

I'm not hidden, My son. I want you to know that the more you live by faith, honoring Me when you cannot see Me; it all the more reinforces the truth of Satan's defeat. How wonderful it is to see him, Satan, more and more defeated by those he defeated in the beginning through deception. Yes, wait on Me, My son. Do not get exasperated or try to take too much upon yourself at one time. My eye is upon you to lead you and guide you and to show you My salvation. My plans are set before you and they will be carried out. In truth, they are already being carried out. All you need do is to set your heart to rest concerning these things."

DAY

14

"...I love the Lord, because He has heard [and now hears] my voice and my supplications. Because He has inclined His ear to me, therefore will I call upon Him as long as I live." PSALM 116:1, 2

MY FATHER AND MY FRIEND

"**B**efore you were born", (the Lord said to me), "**My eyes looked upon and rested upon you, and I took delight at your birth. I knew even before you ever came into the world that you would obey Me. I knew that I would be able to trust you, My son, and ever since you have come to a place in life where you recognize and know My voice, you have proven to yourself that these words of Mine are true. My son, have faith in Me with your whole heart, and believe it when I tell you that you have come a very long way from home and from where you were spiritually in the beginning. I will put you in strategic places as you grow wiser in the knowledge of Who I am, and you will see how My word penetrates the hearts of men, causing them to think twice and even several times about Who I am.**

My son, I have given you insight beyond your years, and this insight has come as a result of your strong and sincere desire for Me, the Lord your God. My son, do not be afraid to know that I am with you, to compliment you, to affirm you and to show you My love continually. You must believe that I am (now) and that I speak to and compliment My children now in this world, where it is most needed. I have high regards for those who call upon Me and expect Me to answer.

Look to Me, My son and trust Me with your whole heart and never shrink back. See, with My own voice I have spoken it before and I will speak it again, I am with you in an unusual way. Yes, it is because I called you to be a prophet from the beginning, but it is for more than that reason that I am with you. I am with you, My son because you truly love Me. You enjoy being with Me and most of your waking hours are spent thinking of Me, your Beloved. My son, before you are beautiful days—days that will bring you pleasure and delight, where you will not be exasperated and sigh and say that you have no pleasure in them, but I, the Lord, yes, even I, the Lord God your Father will restore (all) that was taken from you and I will multiply your (spiritual) seed in the earth.

For out of you, My own dear son will come a generation and then another generation after them because of your obedience to Me. See how gracious I, the Lord am, causing multiple generations to come forth as a result of the obedience of My children. Yes, dear son, I know that you have endured much at the hands of those who have said they love and know Me, when in actuality, they were along for the ride, to get out of Me what they felt would expand their own personal interests.

But because I know all things and I know what is in the heart of every man, I caused a diversion in their plans, My son, and they have not accomplished what they thought they would accomplish. If I am against a man, how can he prosper and succeed in his own way? But as for you, My son, do not hold your head down any longer in sadness and wonder, but know that the days ahead of you are growing brighter. I will give you greater success and men will recognize that you are a prophet, My son, and they will see that I, the Lord, yes, I the Lord, protect you with My very own Presence. See, it is as I have told you, My friend, that My Spirit rests upon you and as you are instructed to speak by Me, your voice will be heard and men will know that you are chosen to walk among them as a brother, a father, a prophet, and as a friend.

You do not need to worry (any more) My son, for I know that the battle scars remain (to some degree) even as My personal scars from the cross remain, but they are there for a purpose. Your scars, My son, for having dealt with men who did not want to honor or obey Me will remind you of the power that I gave you to continue walking among them as well as teach you other things for those you are teaching at the moment.

Write these messages of Mine down and put them in a secret and sensitive place and keep them close to your heart, for in due season you will read them and they will prove to be true in your reading. Although you know they are true at this moment, My son, once I have done many things you will return to this writing and see the faithfulness of the Lord. I will cause all of your enemies to bow down and relent and they will no longer bother or harass you. You will live out your days in peace and prosperity, for I will cause it to happen."

DAY

15

"...I have given and delivered to them Your word (message) and the world has hated them, because they are not of the world [do not belong to the world], just as I am not of the world. I do not ask that You will take them out of the world, but that You will keep and protect them from the evil one. They are not of the world (worldly, belonging to the world), [just] as I am not of the world." JOHN 17:14, 15, 16

My Father, as I come to You today, give me insight into Your will. Help me to better understand how Your good Presence has shaped my life and brought me to the place I am now. I long to be with You, my God, to see You, to be with You personally where I can look upon You and be better acquainted with You by sight. O that my soul should see Your face my God, to bless You, to speak kindly of You to Your face and to share my whole heart with You as I gaze into Your beautiful eyes. You are My Beloved Father, and I have nothing but good things to say to You and nothing but kindness to bestow upon You. How I love You, Jehovah, my God, how I praise and admire You for all of

Your good deeds that You have showered upon me and continue to shower upon me. You are faithful, Father, and there is no other God but You. There is no other Father as You are, My Lord and God, and now You have called me Your friend. Only open my eyes so that I may gaze upon Your beauty more and more. Show me Your revealed Self. Let me see Yourself, Your real Self so that I may be fully satisfied.

"My son, My son, as you have spoken to Me, your Lord and God, I have listened to you. I hear you each time you call out to Me, your Father and Lord and God, and My heart celebrates with joy that you now know Me more intimately. You have gone through many tests and trials and not one of them was unnecessary, but they have caused you to know and recognize Me for the way that I truly am. My son, hold dear to your heart all that you have gone through, and ponder the disappointments and sorrows that have assailed you for many years. Never regret them. For as these tests and trials came by My own hand, they have taught you many things and to understand the nature of man more clearly so that you may speak My word (as I give it to you) to My servants and even those who are not (yet) My servants. You see clearly as I see, but only as I show you what I see—I am the Lord.

My son, see how far I have brought you. With My own hand and My very own Spirit have I led you all these years. You have not been walking about aimlessly in the wilderness, My son, but My hand has been upon you. Listen to Me, know that I am God and know that I am the One Who speaks to you as I did with Moses and with Abraham, sharing My heart and My vision and purpose with you.

See how kind the Lord your God is—I have brought you to a safe place where you can rest and do all that I have put in your heart. I will open your mouth wider, My son, causing it to be filled more and more with My word—My message to My very own children. I have filled you with My Holy Spirit so that you will speak My words to My children. I have given you (through these tests and trials) a compassion and love for people—including and especially those who are unkind, for it is through My (revealed) and personal acts of kindness that I lead people to repentance. You are My vessel, dear son, a vessel of honor and of My own choosing. I enjoy My time with you, and I know that you will always go and do as I instruct you. For My words, (the Lord says), yes, My words are alive and living in your heart. You are faithful, and I do not have to look for another one when I can call upon you, O faithful one. Out of you, My dear son, I, the Lord, will bring forth many.

Because I trust you with what is dear to My very own heart, I will draw men to you and you will speak on My behalf—yes, on My behalf, and then I will draw that one into My very own knowledge, revealing Myself, My real Self to that person, even as I have and will continue to reveal My real Self to you.

My son, never fear—never fear that you are alone or that you are wasting your time, for I, the Lord, yes, I, the Lord am redeeming all that you have done and causing everything you do and have done to return to you (multiplied), so that you will know that I am your God and Father. I will bless you and cause you extreme success (especially) in My own house, for you are called (even) from birth to work in My very own house, and in it, (the Lord says) I have required you to work and in it you shall find rest, peace, consolation, and compassion from those I send you to. For I, the Lord,

(Yes, that is Who I am), I am putting an end to all the (divine) suffering that I caused to come into your life and replacing it with peace and wisdom so that you may be able to express and explain My heart—even My own heart to My people. Rest now, and it will be as I have said, (just as I have told you) that you will never be revisited by the days that I have brought you through. For I have looked and seen for Myself that you have passed the tests that were required by Me so that you could do (and are now doing) the work that I have called you to do before you were born and ever knew of this work."

DAY

16

"...For those who honor Me I will honor..." 1 SAMUEL 2:30

"My son, tell Me what you are thinking. Share your thoughts openly with Me and I will share My thoughts openly with you. I will not hide from you what I am thinking, but I will tell you (face to face) as you are able to listen to what I desire to say. I look for men through whom I might be able to strongly show Myself. I am looking for those who desire to be My vessels of honor. As you cry out to Me, the Lord, I will listen to you. I will cause My ear to hear your words and I will answer you speedily. Do you recognize Who I am, My son? Do you know that I am right here with you and that My hand is laid (to rest) upon you, leading you, guiding you, so that you will be able to find your way in this world. Don't you know that you are of the light now and that the darkness is fleeing from you? Dear son, the more you grow in the knowledge of Who I am, the more you know who you are and what I think about you and how I feel about you. My hand is set upon you steadily, not to do you evil, (the Lord says), but to do good to and through you. Trust this with your whole heart. Run quickly; promote what I say and what I share, so that My people will know that I want to have a personal relationship with them. I want to be involved in their lives. Share with them what I, the Lord your God shares with you, so that they may know what they have in common and what you all have in common with Me as your Father and Lord. Do not be afraid to say what I have said and do not be afraid to share what I have shared, for I, the Lord, yes, I will show that you are My vessel and that I do speak through you. My heart is with those who genuinely obey Me and who genuinely desire to do as I lead them."

DAY

17

"WHEN GOD DOESN'T ANSWER!"

"...Guide me in Your truth and faithfulness and teach me, for You are the God of my salvation; for You [You only and altogether] do I wait [expectantly] all the day long." PSALM 25:5

"...For God alone my soul waits in silence; from Him comes my salvation." PSALM 62:1

"...Unto You do I cry, O Lord my Rock, be not deaf and silent to me, lest, if You be silent to me, I become like those going down to the pit [the grave]." PSALM 28:1

"My child," the Lord spoke to Jennifer. "Why do you act as if you have no God or Helper, when I do not run to your rescue or speak to you when you are in trouble or troubled? Does a mother run to the aid of her child each time the baby cries? Or does the mother begin to recognize the sound of the cry and what that cry demands? My child, I am with you—right here—I never leave you—I will never abandon you—I am wide awake. I do not slumber nor sleep. I, the Lord am with you, watching you so that you will learn to know Who I am and how I do things. For this is what the Lord your God says to you, Jennifer. Listen to Me and pay close attention to what I tell you, My daughter; when I am not actively engaged in speaking with you, it does not mean that I am unconcerned or do not care about where you are or what you are going through. I am aware of every breath that you take and every step that you take.

Many times you have felt that you were all alone because I did not speak to you or did not lead you in a certain way that you felt I should have. My dear one, learn to know that I am with you wherever you are and wherever you go. You never escape my eye. If I am not speaking to you, then ask Me if there is a reason why and I will tell you. I will speak to you clearly, giving you insight into what you do not know or understand. I oftentimes do not speak so that you will be given the opportunity to (stretch) your faith. I do not want you to try to predict what I will do or assume that I will do the same things I have done in the past as I've communicated with you. My desire is that your faith develops and grows strong so that when you feel alone or when Satan attacks or when circumstances contradict what you believe I have spoken, you will (stand) upon not only what I have spoken but upon the (reputation) I have established with you.

My dear one, do not allow your imagination to deceive you. For when you begin to imagine that I am speaking or that I have spoken and are not sure that I have or am speaking to you, it opens up the door for deception, not so much from Satan, dear one, but through your own wandering mentally about what I may or may not have said or may or may not do. Satan is a strategist and an opportunist. He will take advantage of what you are uncertain about or do not believe and use it against you. But be wise, dear one, even as he is wise in using deception—be wise in (waiting) and listening for My voice so that you will indeed know what I have spoken and speak it back to your own mind and to Satan! Hear Me, I, the Lord will instruct you. When you are at your weakest, do not despise it, but accept it; embrace it dear one, until you realize and know the power you have with Me when you are weak.

The problem often with your wanting to hear Me is that you sometimes only call upon Me when (you) feel or are weak, but My power and sufficiency is always the same, meeting you at your faith level. Have faith in Me, dear Jennifer, and not in your ability to have faith in what you believe about Me. I am the Lord—I am of (age). I have been alive for a very long time, and I am very much aware of where you are and am able to (save) you when necessary.

"But what do I do, My Lord, to stop this fear that I feel when I cannot sense that You are near me, to speak to me, to help me, especially when I am weak and need for You to speak to me? What do I do then, Lord? Am I wrong for needing You to speak to me?"

"No dear one, you are not wrong for needing Me to speak to you. The problem comes when you desire for Me to speak to you so badly that you (create) words in your own mind that I am not speaking, even though the words may resemble the things that I could or would actually speak to you Myself. You must learn the difference between My voice and your own soul speaking to you.

I know dear one that when you are afraid, lonely, feeling weak and forgotten, the tendency is to reach inward (within yourself) to find Me, but I am within you and outside and even all around you, nothing subjects Me or keeps Me penned in—I am the Lord! You must know that I am not contained in your mind, but I, the Lord, live within your spirit. That is where I am, and when you need Me, My voice shall be heard, but know this as truth, dear Jennifer, I know what you need far better than you do and when you need it.

I will speak to you when I (get ready) so that your faith will be based upon what I tell you (at the moment) or what I have shared, and not what your soul is demanding of Me at the moment. Don't think unkindly of Me when I do not (run) to your rescue when you believe you need Me the most. I am right alongside you, right here with you, and I know when you are truly in trouble or when you need for Me to speak to you. I will speak to you so that you will have the faith to meet the challenge.

So do not be alarmed or disheartened, dear one, I am right here, but know for sure that your courage and strength and your faith are built during the times when you are hurting the most, not when everything is going well with you. Call to Me and I will answer you, dear one, but allow Me to answer in My own time, for just as a child begins to recognize (after a while) that the mother is not going to come with a certain noise or cry he makes, so will you begin to learn the difference between when you need for Me to come (to reveal) Myself, and when you can simply use your knowledge of Me—that which has been built through our conversing together and My revealing Myself to you, to know that I am with you. This kind of unshakable knowledge will keep you strong, dear one, and you will realize the difference between My own voice and your soul speaking to you. Then you will know that I am God the way that I intend to be known in your life."

DAY

18

"…O Lord, You have heard the desire and the longing of the humble and oppressed; You will prepare and strengthen and direct their hearts, You will cause Your ear to hear." PSALM 10:17

"…I love You fervently and devotedly, O Lord, my Strength. The Lord is my Rock, my Fortress, and my Deliverer; my God, my keen and firm Strength in Whom I will trust and take refuge, my Shield, and the Horn of my salvation, my High tower." PSALM 18:1, 2

"…Now I know that the Lord saves His anointed; He will answer him from His holy heaven with the saving strength of His right hand." PSALM 20:6

O my Lord and my great Strength, I will call on You for as long as I live. With my final breath in this life, may it praise and honor You for all that You have done for me. For You have known me, affirmed me, addressed me by name and set me apart so that I may progressively know and understand Your will to fulfill it in this life. How I love You, O Lord, My God: How

I treasure each moment with You because You have listened and heard me and come to my defense. No wonder the Angels cry out to You, saying, "Holy, Holy, Holy." I am in awe of You, My God. May my continued prayer be to know You, to recognize You in everyday life and to not put faith in my faith or my ability to believe You. For, O Lord, my God, You have caused me to know You, to see inside Your heart—to want it, need it, desire it, recommend it, and to embrace it. For You, O Lord my God are a Rewarder to those who genuinely seek You out and genuinely want and desire You. You will not hide nor keep Yourself from being visible to them. How I love You, O Lord, as You have treated me with the utmost kindness. So my thoughts constantly turn to You even as Your thoughts turn to me. How good it is that we, Your children, have a God and Father like You—One Who constantly has us in mind.

"...My son," the Lord spoke to me. **"I hear you and I accept your words, for they are refreshing and uplifting, and words that are true. You are not speaking something that you have heard or read in a book, but the words that you are sharing are true about Me and your relationship with Me; for you have seen Me, the Lord, (Yes, the Lord your God), as I truly am and the way that I want to be seen. My true son, one after My own heart, continue to lay your entire being on Me—all that you desire—all that you believe you desire, and I will show you the right way.**

Believe Me with all of your heart when I tell you this: 'My plans include you, and all that I am thinking of include those who genuinely follow and desire Me. Although for a very short time—yes, a very short time you have been in what seems to be a wilderness period, I have observed you and you have not found fault with Me,

the Lord, neither in words or how you personally think of Me. I have kept My eyes upon you and I see that your heart is pure towards Me, and you have (yet again) passed the testing of your faith. I require you to be a man of power, authority, strength, grace, and one who knows the Lord and is able to describe Me as I am.

Surely, you have walked with Me and I have shown My nature to you as you have laid down your own life and chosen the life that I chose for you before you were born. I am the Lord and beside Me there is no other God—Jehovah, that is Who I am, and My Name is written upon you, setting you apart, causing you to be distinguished in My very own eyes. Do not be afraid My dear beloved son, for as you continue to stretch your eyes toward Me, seeking Me as you would daily food and water, I will reveal Myself—showing you in detail, yes, intimate detail, Who I am and who you are.

Do not be afraid, I say to you, do not be afraid if it seems you are losing the things that you have in this world, for all that I require of you, I, the Lord, will return it multiplied, just as you have seen in the past. For if you do not allow the things of this world—including what you desire the most and even the things I have personally promised you—to draw you away from Me, you will receive them in due time. I will not keep anything good from you. I am the Lord."

DAY

19

"WHAT DO WE DO WHEN WHAT GOD SAYS SEEMS TO CONTRADICT WHAT WE SEE AND FEEL?"

"After these things, the word of the Lord came to Abram in a vision, saying, Fear not, Abram, I am your Shield, your abundant compensation, and your reward shall be exceedingly great. And Abram said, Lord God, what can You give me, since I am going on [from this world] childless and he who shall be the owner and heir of my house is this [steward] Eliezer of Damascus? And Abram continued, Look, You have given me no child; and [a servant] born in my house is my heir. And behold, the word of the Lord came to him, saying, This man shall not be your heir, but he who shall come from your own body shall be your heir. And He brought him outside [his tent into the starlight] and said, Look now toward the heavens and count the stars—if you are able to number them. Then He said to him, So shall your descendants be." GENESIS 15:1-5

Dear Beloved Children of God, many of us often try to (understand) God when He speaks to us. Understanding often comes later after (acceptance) of what God has said, whether we readily receive it or not. Often, the question becomes "How can I accept something I do not understand?" We have been operating for many years in accepting what the world feeds us, though we never understand exactly what is going on. However, this is not true with God. In our walk with Jesus, we are to "listen" for His voice. Jesus appeared as man to men, however, in the day we live, the Spirit that was in Jesus' (flesh); the One Who has always existed abode and found His housing in the flesh of Jesus, just as it was spoken to Mary. The Spirit of God (lived) in Jesus, and now that same Presence of God lives within our flesh and has and continues to make His abode as well as reveals Himself to and through us as we accept Him. Now, I do want to be sure that we all understand together that God speaks about "future" events when He speaks to us. Often He is talking about the "not" yet in the present tense, which can be conflicting and confusing to one who is trying to "figure" God out. When God speaks this way dear friends, He is trying to train us to be (creative) and to understand His creative power. He does this by "revealing" it to us—by showing us what is going to happen in the future.

We were created by God to dream and to have goals that find their origin with Him. Oftentimes, however, we try to "press" past what God is speaking to us to get more insight; however, we must understand that God (always) speaks specifically. He says exactly what He wants to say and what He means. It may (never) be what we want or wish He would say to us, but God is trying to work with us by changing our minds in His conversation with us.

We often speak to God about what we "want," and seldom listen to Him about what He wants. Herein lies many of our troubles. Whenever God is speaking to us, even though He may (never) say anything in regards to what we are troubled about, His conversation includes our concerns. We are limited by what we see, think, and feel, based upon our current situations. However, Jesus was able to (walk through) and live through what was happening at the current moment—no matter how difficult things were—because He said this: "The Son does only what He sees the Father doing." Jesus knew that what the Father was planning included the way out of whatever was confronting Him—that is why, when we learn to observe Jesus' Spirit operating within us, we can (see) past what is in front of us, hindering us, or physically limiting us.

If we listen to His Spirit, truly listen to His voice and accept what He is saying, we learn that God is in control. Nothing that forms itself against us prevails as we are restored to the (mental) intellectual understanding that God is with us, that He is living within our flesh—the same way He lived in Jesus' flesh, and the same way He (cooperated) with all those who came before Jesus who believed in Him. It does not matter where faith found its origin (Old or New) Testament because believing in the Old is the same as believing in the New. God honors faith.

We must grow to the point of (living) in God's Presence, where He is able to speak to us regularly. Although He (will) say things we do not understand and find hard to believe, His goal in doing so is to bring us up to a (level) of higher understanding, knowledge, and reasoning. He is trying to get us to stop being limited by the "sight" realm. This is why Sarah pushed ahead of God's will and accomplished her own will in bringing forth Ishmael. She was looking at her physical limitations, rather than (sticking) to and adhering to what God had spoken concerning bearing a son herself.

Whenever God speaks to you, (listen) to what He says. Stay within the perimeters of what He has shared. Although this will take a faith fight, it will also mean victory in the end. God causes our faith to grow by speaking and sharing with us what He knows. This is intended to bring us into a faith walk and communion with Him that goes beyond what we see, think, and feel. This new walk of faith of the Lord's is intended to change what we see; and if what we see is changed by God's faithfulness, then what we feel and think will also change. In other words, all of God's words are true, all of them, thus exercising true righteousness within our thought processes. A battle comes because we have listened to Satan's lies for so long that we believe untruths about Jesus. Thus it is hard for us to accept that God is consistently good and that He is actually speaking (good) things to us. We must eventually get to the point where we accept that neither our goodness or any good deeds that we may perform have nothing to do with God's eternal goodness and favor that He shows us. In fact, it is His constant (revelation) of Himself to us that leads us to repentance—or (righteous) living by experience with Him—the revelation of Himself. As we see Him as His Revealed Self, it gives us the option to change. I say option because some of us are not willing to wait on God's plans for us or His timing. This is what happened to Israel—they weren't willing to wait on God's promises concerning them.

Remember dear child of God that Satan is in a mad race to control all of us in the thought realm, for this is the place where we feel things. We feel contrary to what God says and those feelings never allow us to find a landing and solid place in God. However, if we begin to embrace the thoughts of God—we will experience an altogether different battle—a winnable battle because our promise is in Christ. We cannot win such a battle if we continue to hold on to what we feel and think which is opposite to what God is saying and where He is taking us.

The emotionally healthy person is the one who continues to feed from the thoughts of God. Sometimes God may speak in strange or dark speech, but this is because we do not recognize it is actually our thoughts that are alien, not His! We have grown accustomed to accepting what feels good to our hearts and minds, rather than accepting the truth of God into our minds and hearts. Yes, dear ones, when we accept the message that the Spirit of God speaks, we will begin to understand that we have new flesh that is acceptable to God. The new flesh is our new nature—the nature given us by the Spirit—enabling our human spirit to engage in holy communion with our Savior, Jesus. He will show us the way that we are to go by His Spirit that lives within us. However, remember, that unless we accept Him at His Word, we are not abiding with Him, and if that is the case, we will continue to walk around Him, avoiding direct contact and communion with Him and never understanding or receiving His plans for our lives. Now, when we surrender ourselves to this Great Messiah Whose Name is Holy, Life, Redeemer, we are able to see His purposes more clearly. However, we will suffer tests and trials, but these tests and trials are appropriated to us by God, so we will be able to bear up under them by His grace. After we have suffered for a little while, more of our Father is revealed; and we feel differently, understanding more and more that our thoughts are becoming like His.

As we regain our righteous minds, we will begin to understand that God is trying to restore the mind Satan robbed from us, which was in constant fellowship with God. So dear ones, do not grow weary in doing right or righteous things that God Himself has chosen for us to do. Don't stop suffering prematurely, but let it have its full work in us, so at the end of this suffering, Christ will be more visible. Christ is already with us, however He is sometimes hard to see and hear because our lives have been shaped by this world and the culture in which we live. Our Father has created a new world for us to enjoy right now in His Presence. So don't be earthbound, but instead be bound to His Spirit and His power, which will bring glorious liberty to keep us in the world but not held prisoner to it.

DAY

20

It was raining that afternoon when I decided to take a walk. For a while I had been struggling with depression and discouragement. Something wasn't right. My life was going well. The job was going well, my ministry, I thought, was good, and my fiancé and I were doing well and coming along well with marriage plans, but something inside my heart wasn't right. I had been so busy lately, squeezing in quiet time when I could, and trying my best to meet ministry deadlines and to finish ministry projects, but it seemed as if my love for what I was doing for God was diminishing. Even though I was gong to church every Sunday and some Wednesdays, it seemed as if these visits only made the emptiness more apparent and the noise in my heart seemed to grow louder. I cannot say that I was led by the Lord to walk that afternoon, but I felt compelled to get out—even in the rain, to walk away from the demands on my life that never seemed to end. While I did not plan on talking to the Lord, I just wanted to think, to sort out some things, after all, I was supposed to marry soon, so shouldn't I be happier? The sadness, discouragement, and depression that I was feeling was not coming from my wedding plans, but something deeper, something that I could not put my finger on. While walking that day, with the rain pouring steadily down, I sat on a bench in the park to think. Yes, the bench was wet, but I didn't care. I kept under my umbrella and simply tried to get peace in my cluttered mind.

"**What are you doing?**" I heard a voice say.

"What?" was my answer.

"**I asked, what are you doing?**"

Before I answered this time, I pondered the idea that I was imagining things or that this could be the Holy Spirit speaking to me. I grew up in the charismatic church so I am familiar with the way God speaks and that He does speak. The sad thing is that I had not heard from Him in so long.

"What do You mean, what am I doing?" I asked, then looked around me only to find an empty park with cars steadily passing by on the highway a short distance from me."

"**What are you doing with the life that I've given you?**" Then without question, I knew that it was the Lord. Surprised to some degree, I simply composed myself and for a moment, the confusion, depression, and discouragement seemed to leave. Finally, I had a settled mind.

"Well, Lord," I began my response. "I am going to church. I am doing well with the ministry that I feel You've called me to do. I am giving a lot more than I ever have, and things seem to be going well with my current ministry projects."

"**Are you happy about these things?**" the Lord asked. "**Are you satisfied with yourself—just you, with who you are as I've defined you?**"

"What?" I asked. "I don't understand the question."

"**That's why I asked you what you were doing,**" the Lord said.

"Why would I ask you what are you doing?"

I knew God knew what I was doing. He was asking me because I didn't know myself. I was lost in my mind, but I hadn't given it much thought before now.

"Have I asked you to do the things you are doing, or are you doing them on your own? Why are you doing these things?"

"Well, Lord, I'm doing them because I feel that these are areas where I am talented, skilled, and where I do well in every day life."

"True," the Lord said to me. "You are very talented and skilled. Jesus was a carpenter, but when it was time for Him to do what He was put into the earth to do publicly, He left that behind. Could you leave what you are doing behind?"

I felt terrified at the very thought. Didn't God understand that what I was doing was part of who I am...or were my activities defining me as a Christian in my own eyes?

"Son, you are wearing yourself out doing things for Me, rather than getting to know Who I am. All of these things you are doing are good things, but not necessarily the right things. They are not necessarily the things I've chosen for you to do, although they are good things. What would make them right for you and satisfying as you do them, is knowing that I've chosen them for you. But doing things within themselves because they are good things will soon wear you out, depress you, and discourage you, just like you feel now. You cannot define who you are by doing what you do in My kingdom. Much like the message doesn't describe the one who actually brings it—it represents the heart of the one who sends it. Of course, what you are doing brings some personal satisfaction to you for a while because you feel closer to Me in your activity, correct?"

"Yes, Lord," I said, feeling somewhat challenged and looking for another emotional direction to go into. It seemed as if the Lord was addressing the source of the sorrow that brought me to the park on such a rainy day.

"I do not want you to spend all of your life doing things for Me. I will give you opportunities to do things, but I desire more than anything else for you to come to know Me—not to do things for Me. My Son, Adam got to know Me through our fellowship together, and I simply gave Him things to do. He did not get his identity from what he did in the Garden, but his identity and self worth came from his spending intimate time with Me. Adam's heart was open to Me. He did not hide it from Me during those beginning days we shared together, so I was His ultimate influence. You need to be influenced more by being with Me. Don't worry. I know that you are afraid that you may not hear Me clearly. I understand that you try to be a perfectionist."

"Then why am I hearing You so clearly now?"

"Because you have been looking for Me. You came out here to the park looking for something, and I simply showed up to make it clear that you are looking for Me. You are trying to find out what to do in life and even with your life, and I am the One Who brings definition to the things you do. I can assure you that I am not requiring you to do all of the ministry things that you are doing. I want you to spend time with Me—if you do, then you will recognize My voice, My Spirit, and the Scriptures will read better. You will see Me in the Scriptures and sense Me operating in your life regularly. You will feel My Presence and have fellowship with Me.

You are not called to do ministry—not the way that you think. Ministry is something that a person is designated to do by My leading and input. It is not something you choose to do simply because it will make you somehow fit into My Church. Some men are not called to do any ministry at all—not publicly.

For some, ministry is simply doing good things for others, because I have done good things for the individual who does good things for others. He is simply responding to others in the way that I have responded to Him, in kindness. These are things that so few notice as being ministry—simply loving and caring for others naturally. If you will wait on Me—wait—don't be in such a hurry. I am not programmed by this world. I am not in any hurry. You have been in a hurry because you do not see the reason to wait. My son, dear son, listen to Me; if you will look to Me for your complete satisfaction in and for all things, then the reason why you are waiting for Me will become clearer and you will not feel that you are wasting time. Then impatience will lose its power over you.

So, you are called to know Me—not to do things for Me. I know with your dutiful makeup that it will take time for you to understand what I am saying. But do as I instruct you to do. Go now…go back home and sit with Me for a while, just like you are doing now. Sometimes I may not say anything to you. It may not be necessary. But My silence does not mean punishment or My disinterest in you. I could be training you to be patient in My silence. Stop looking for ministry, dear son, and it will find you in your intimate times with Me. So many people are running to other countries, trying to feed the poor, looking for demons to cast out, and trying to establish shelters for the poor. While there is nothing wrong with these things, dear son, a man's primary call is to know Who I am.

The reason why Jesus came was to bring back—to restore you, yes, you and everyone like you, back to Myself—to be in full fellowship with Me, and in that fellowship—that holy relationship, ministry, if any at all, will come. For the time being, dear son, seek Me, only Me, and out of that intimacy, you will find Me, hear Me, and I will make Myself clear in time. Some men are confused about what they are doing, even in ministry. They are confused because they are not sure that they are hearing from Me about what they are doing, but wouldn't it be wise to hear clearly from the Instructor before beginning a project that you assume is for or from Him?

"...Let be and be still, and know (recognize and understand) that I am God." PSALM 46:10A

"...I love those who love me, and those who seek me early and diligently shall find me." PROVERBS 8:17

"...Then you will seek Me, inquire for, and require Me [as a vital necessity] and find Me when you search for Me with all your heart. I will be found by you, says the Lord..." JEREMIAH 29:13, 14A

DAY

21

"...My soul, wait only upon God and silently submit to Him; for my hope and expectation are from Him." PSALM 62:5

"...In the morning You hear my voice, O Lord; in the morning I prepare [a prayer, a sacrifice] for You and watch and wait [for You to speak to my heart]." PSALM 5:3

"...In my distress [when seemingly closed in] I called upon the Lord and cried to my God; He heard my voice out of His temple (heavenly dwelling place), and my cry came before Him, into His [very] ears." PSALM 18:6

Father, I position myself to hear You...to listen to You. I calmly kneel here, waiting on You to speak to me. I know that if You will speak to me, dear Lord, the worry and fear and uncertainty that I have will ease. For I know that if You will speak to me, whether You choose to address what I am concerned about or not, I know that You will have heard me. I come in confidence, dear Father, based upon the certainty of Your words to me, knowing that You listen, knowing that You hear, and knowing that

You will answer me. I will not doubt my God's ability to speak to me and to set the record straight, whether that be in my own heart, or to give me insight into what I do not know. Do listen, dear Father, my Friend (as You have called me), and give me wisdom, delight, and joy, in knowing that You have listened to me and kindly shown regards toward my petition. I have no other God but You, dear Father, no other idol or thing has my attention—I long to be with You all the day long, and as a result (of my setting my priorities) in order, there is nothing that hides Your face or the sensing of Your will from me. Father, my soul is disquieted within me and I sense nowhere to put my feet at this time. Listen and hear me, dear Jehovah (my Father), and tell me, where are You taking me?

> *"...The earnest (heartfelt, continued) prayer of a righteous man makes tremendous power available [dynamic in its working]."*
> *JAMES 5:16B*

"My son," the Lord spoke to me. **"Know (without doubting) that I hear you—that I listen to you when you call to Me. I hear you (each and every time) and without fail. My eyes are upon you— waiting and listening to and for your voice, for you have been trained by Me personally, yes, by Me, (the Lord), personally, to speak out of your spirit, rather than out of your fears. For as you call out to Me (deliberately) and in truth, you can be certain that I will hear and that I will answer you, and that I will set your thoughts into action, giving you the ability to move from one place to another, having received wisdom from listening to Me. Now, I will listen to you, dear son, but you must also listen to Me. For what makes a man's prayer powerful is not his faithfulness and belief in his prayer or My**

ability to answer it alone, but it is also in his ability to hear back, to receive back from Me that which I choose to speak. For I will respond to you in righteousness, satisfying the righteous desire and need within you for Myself. Hear Me, for I am Jehovah—the First and the Last—the Beginning and the Ending—the Alpha and the Omega—the One Who has always been alive, and I continue to live as I am. You have found it difficult to find a footing or a place to feel comfortable or to feel as if you belong in the world, because you are growing to be more knowledgeable of Who I am. I am revealing more and more of Myself to you, and as I do, there is a drawing (rapturing) upward of your spirit to Me. And as this happens, dear one, it causes inner conflict within your soul. But do not let this bother you, dear son, for I, the Lord am teaching you what it means (by definition) to be in the world but not to be controlled by it. I understand dear son that this can be a bit confusing for you, even causing you to feel alienated and estranged from your friends and family, but it is My will that you should know Me more intimately and clearly.

As you continue to yield to Me, you will find that the fear of not knowing where you are or where you are going will disappear. Although this has been a trying time for you, dear son, you are reaching and calling out to Me more genuinely, purely, and of necessity. For I am the Way and I am the Truth and I am the Life Giver. I will make Myself plain to you in every avenue of life, teaching you how to think soberly and clearly at all times. For do not allow this temporary place of not understanding fully what I am doing in your life to cause you to stumble or fear, only continue to seek Me out, just as you are doing now—which establishes My Name in you and in those who believe the testimony that is developing in your life from Christ. For although it may seem strange, this walk that I have you on, I assure you that it will lead to greater power, understanding, and a clearer ability to reveal Who I am to others. Not all men are called to do what you do, dear one, but if you will listen to Me, (yes, listen to Me, the Lord) with all of your heart, then I will keep your mind at ease and at peace."

And then I accepted His words to me. I began to feel the enveloping of His peace—His rest. Sometimes as we walk the pathway that God has chosen for us, it seems lonely, as if no one else is walking along the same pathway, but we can be assured, that God knows the way that He has chosen for us and that He will lead us directly and clearly, until we become so acquainted with Him and His way of doing things, that we welcome His ways, and begin to live them out, for God desires us to walk as He walks.

"...For I have kept the ways of the Lord and have not wickedly departed from my God." PSALM 18:21

"...As for God, His way is perfect! The word of the Lord is tested and tried; He is a shield to all those who take refuge and put their trust in Him." PSALM 18:30

"...Show me Your ways, O Lord; teach me Your paths." PSALM 25:4

"...The steps of a [good] man are directed and established by the Lord when He delights in his way [and He busies Himself with his every step]." PSALM 37:23

22

"...As for me, I will call upon God, and the Lord will save me. Evening and morning and at noon will I utter my complaint and moan and sigh, and He will hear my voice. He has redeemed my life in peace from the battle that was against me [so that none came near me], for they were many who strove with me." PSALM 55:16-18

"...With my voice I cry to the Lord, and He hears and answers me out of His holy hill..." PSALM 3:4

Early in the morning will I come before You, my God, Whose Name is the Lord. I will comfort, quiet and position myself to listen to and for Your voice, to hear what is on Your heart, so that my heart may be satisfied by the sound of Your voice—the voice of Your wisdom and so that I may gain insight, my Father, to know You more intimately, so that I may delight myself all the more in You. When I call to You, my Lord, my exceeding and great Reward, please listen to me, my Father, and do not delay to speak with me—face to face. Speak if You are willing, so that I may be satisfied with the appearance of Your glory. Do not hide Yourself from me, my Lord, but show Yourself clearly, that I may know You more diversely, expecting only righteousness and what is right from You. Do not allow me to be disappointed as I kneel here before You, Jehovah, my God, but speak to me—feeding me, so that I may be satisfied this day. For from Your lips come the words that lead to eternal life—that cause me to engage with You in everyday living, so that I may know how to live in this world, until I see You in Your complete, revealed form. So I sat and I waited to hear the voice of the Lord.

"Do not be afraid," the Lord said to me, and I rested, positioning myself so that He might be able to speak more deeply, keeping nothing from me, even if some of what He said might be hard to hear.

"I love you, dear son," He said. **"My son, the hour has come that I will begin to reveal more of Myself to My people—though My Spirit is well poured out among My people, sadly, not all of them will hear Me or recognize Me, for their desires are more for this world and what is in the world rather than My own nature. A man will always hold on to what is important to him; however, if a man will relinquish what he considers his rights, then I will give him his rights, causing him to know more intimately who he is in My sight. However, if a man does not fully come to Me, he will never recognize Who I am nor the time of My divine visitation. These things will remain estranged from him. Sit here with Me, my son, (the Lord said to me), and as you are more and more able to believe Me, I will show you more of Myself. You cannot see within My Person (My face), My goodness, and not see what I am about to do, for I have the power to show you what has not been created (for you) yet, if you are willing to see it. I have said this: 'There is no fear in**

love, but perfect love casts out all fear,' and if you are afraid of what will happen or what I may do to you, My son, then My love is not yet perfected in you. Where there is perfect love, there is no room for fear—it is completely done away with. That is why I want you to come in before Me and lay down yourself—your very life, the person you are, so that I may reveal to you (inwardly) Who I am. I promise, I will not allow anything that is needful for you to know to remain hidden, but I will reveal Myself to you and show Myself to you in the areas where you need to see and know Me, and then you will know Me by experience.

You do not need to fear or be anxious about anything. I already know what is going to happen, and you are included in My plans. My son, never think that being in My Presence—being alone with Me is a waste of your time—for I am the (time giver), and I will restore to you, yes, I will give back to you and even redeem any time you feel that you have wasted. I am the Lord God, and no one—no one can do the things that I can do, and you will see My glory—yes, Myself, if you continue to obey Me.

Dear son, know with all of your heart (the Lord said to me), that you cannot understand what I have not given you the ability to understand; however, as you continue to seek Me, the Lord, with your whole heart, I will show Myself to you and what My plans are, I will reveal those to you. Your life, My son, (yes), even your natural life is in Me, for I am and have become both man and God, essentially, so that you may know Me in your humanity.

For I want to reveal and to show Myself to you, just the way that I am, but you must know, My son, that this knowledge and revelation comes measure by measure. For as you look upon Me, as you gaze upon My face, seeing Myself, parts of you will die daily, but you must remember there is no death with Me unless there is also resurrection. Don't be afraid, even in times of famine or when things are out of your control—they never were really in your control, as I keep a careful and watchful eye upon you at all times. And if you will listen to Me, listen for Me, and wait for Me, I will come and visit with you, revealing what is to come to you, and satisfy your need and desire to know things, and cause your heart to be at peace."

> *"...Behold, the Lord's eye is upon those who fear Him [who revere and worship Him with awe], who wait for Him and hope in His mercy and loving-kindness, To deliver them from death and keep them alive in famine. Our inner selves wait [earnestly] for the Lord; He is our Help and our Shield."* PSALM 33:18, 19, 20

> *"...For this God is our God forever and ever; He will be our guide [even] until death."* PSALM 48:14

DAY

23

"LEARN FROM THE SILENCE."

"...But know that the Lord has set apart for Himself [and given distinction to] him who is godly [the man of loving-kindness]. The Lord listens and heeds when I call to Him." PSALM 4:3

"...For I know the thoughts and plans that I have for you, says the Lord, thoughts and plans for welfare and peace and not for evil, to give you hope in your final outcome." JEREMIAH 29:11

"...Then those who feared the Lord talked often one to another; and the Lord listened and heard it, and a book of remembrance was written before Him of those who reverenced and worshipfully feared the Lord and who thought on His name." MALACHI 3:16

"**M**y son, it is a good thing for you to pursue Me, to look for Me everyday of your life. But you do not have to pursue and look for Me as if I am hiding. As you look for Me with your whole heart, just as you have been doing and just as I have taught you, you will find Me. I will come out into the open—I will reveal Myself to you, even to your thought processes so that you may be able to know what My will is. You will not always be given a timeline by Me, My son, but do not allow that to bother, worry, or trouble you. Do not become anxious by what you have no control over. For the more you grow in your knowledge of Who I am, the more you will understand that there is nothing that happens that I do not see or am not aware of.

I do protect those who walk with Me, My son. Those who have a special interest in Me, those who lay their natural lives aside and seek for Me, not for blessings, honor, or to be distinguished in the eyes of men. To those who genuinely look for Me, the Lord, I set them into My own personal plans just as I did with Adam, and in this process of their working with Me, I show them My glory— My essence, My Person. I reveal to them My nakedness and in the midst of this revealed glory, they see Me as I am.

Surely, My son, just as I have told you, no man can see Me as I am and continue to walk in the natural. Such a man begins to die to what he is and takes up what he has become as a result of the shed blood of the First-born from the dead, Whose Name is Jesus, Righteous, Holy, the Extreme and ultimate Gift to mankind. He is the Savior of this world, and there is no other (First-born) Son Who has been given for this divine and holy purpose.

Trust it, My son, and believe what I tell you with your whole heart. I realize that some of the things that I share with you are hard to believe and understand, but I always tell you the truth and I will explain Myself, if you are willing to listen. For I have created mankind so that I may fellowship with My creation—that My creation should know Me and that I should commune with that

. which I have created—namely man. I say to you this day, My son, do not pursue what is in your heart that will cause you to lose sight of Me, your Father, but pursue what I put in your heart to pursue—allow My words and My will to be at the forefront of your heart and always before your eyes. If you will do this, then you will also find what your will is—what your will should have been from the beginning, had Adam and Eve never dishonored the words I gave them to keep.

Be careful to listen to Me, My son, not out of fear or dread of what might happen to you if you do not listen, but out of reverence and out of love. For you have seen with your own eyes and know with your own heart that as you listen to Me, I will always reveal and show you the truth behind what I say. Never allow the cares or concerns that you have in this world to rob you of your joy or your fellowship with Me, although the things of this world, the concerns and demands that are in this world will always compete with your time with Me, your Father.

However, My son, know that just as Mary sat at My feet and found what was necessary for that moment and for the days to come, there is no better place for you than at My feet, listening to what I have to tell you. I will give you insight that will protect and cover your heart and keep you from being afraid. I will wash your mind and clear it as you sit with Me, expressing My heart and giving you insight into what you do not know and giving you a better understanding of what you do know. Yes, I am the Lord your God and the God of My people, those who genuinely call out to Me and expect Me to answer.

Have no agenda, My son, have nothing set in place that proves to push you away from Me and out of My Presence—what you do not know, if it is needed, I will share it with you—I will reveal it to you. You have no need to be desperate, for I, the Lord, yes, I have everything under control, and even when things do not go the way that you expect them to, never look puzzled or confused, wondering, where is the Lord.

Am I not with you? Am I not here standing beside you, My son and My friend? Do I leave you when things become difficult or when your emotions are vexed and you do not know the answer? Surely, there are times when I will not speak, but it is never with the intention to punish or to push you away from Me. Learn from the silence, My son, what can be heard in it! If you will listen to your own heart in times when I am quiet, then you will hear wisdom coming forth from the depths of your heart—wisdom that has been gained from your time with Me.

My son, although I speak well with you, you cannot glean all that I am saying at once. For My knowledge—the knowledge of the holy is captured as you see Me as I am, for it is not words alone that you are hearing, My son, but you are engaging with the Lord your God—the One and only True God, the One Who has been alive forever. Do not rush or be in a hurry. I am with you—to console you, to rescue you, to feed you from My very own lips so that you may spend each day satisfied in My Presence."

24

"...*For the Lord your God has blessed you in all the work of your hand. He knows your walking through this great wilderness. These forty years the Lord your God has been with you; you have lacked nothing.*" DEUTERONOMY 2:7

"...*And you shall [earnestly] remember all the way which the Lord your God led you these forty years in the wilderness, to humble you and to prove you, to know what was in your [mind and] heart, whether you would keep His commandments or not.*" DEUTERONOMY 8:2

My Father and My God, out of all the people I have known, I have never met anyone like You. For so many years I did not know that my heart longed to hear the Truth, to hear it spoken. Within me, from the beginning, within all of Your people, my Lord, I believe You have put within us the desire to know the Truth. And as I have walked with You for these few years that I have, I have found that the Truth is a Person Whose Name is Jesus—the First born of many brothers, Whom You gave to us so that we might know the truth from Your lips in bodily form, from Someone Who knows You, from Someone Who has known You from the very beginning and was willing to come into this world as Your personal representative. My Lord and my God, I cannot think of anyone so excellent, so trustworthy and true, Who would come and give His life so perfectly. But the more I live and the more I grow to know You as You reveal Yourself, the more I understand how kind You are and that You have had a very personal plan for us—Your creation from the very beginning. Oh, dear Lord, today my prayer is that I will continue in this walk that You have shown and given and prepared for me. Help me not to stray from the way that You have provided for me.

Although I realize that there will be trials and tests, I am also convinced that You are with me—of this one thing I am completely sure, that You are with me, have been with me, and that You will not fail me. I trust You, my Lord. I long to be with You, to see You, to embrace You, and to gaze into Your beauty. While I realize that my life has often been filled with bad circumstances, as we all have our share, I have come to know that there is nothing that forms itself against me that succeeds, especially as I keep my focus on You. I have tasted that portion of Yourself, my Father and Lord that You have afforded me, and I have seen with my own eyes that You are consistently good.

From the beginning when You first began to introduce Yourself to me and to make Yourself known, I have begun to recognize You and begun to want to be more like You, My Father. O, come to me, my Lord, and reveal Yourself. For in the darkest hours that I have faced, times when I did not know what to do and times when I did not know if I was going to make it, You came through to save me, to help me and to assist me. Thank You for being so kind.

I open my entire life to You, my precious Father because I know that You are with me, that You listen to me and that You have concern for me that no one else is able to have. You care for all of us, Your people, in ways that we cannot begin to understand or know; however, if we were to yield ourselves, to learn from the Scriptures the things that You have made plain to us, to open our eyes so that You may be revealed, we would see You in ways that we have never seen or known.

How I trust You, my Father, and that with my whole heart. For that which I did not know or comprehend with a fallen mind, You have revealed by coming out into the open, sharing Your heart, giving me Your thoughts and teaching me Your ways. So now I see You—not as I did originally—but as the Person You have revealed Yourself to be.

"From the very beginning, My eyes have been upon you, My son, and I knew that at a certain time, you would come to Me—to be with Me. And I knew that when you saw Me the way that I truly am, you would change your mind about Me. I am called Jehovah— the One and True Living God—the Lord, that is Who I am. I am more than willing to show Myself—to reveal Myself—and to give Myself away to those who are willing to listen to Me, to believe Me, to want to be with Me—even as I want to be with My own creation.

For just as I have intimate and unbridled fellowship with the Son and the Holy Spirit, so do I want unbridled and unhindered fellowship with man—how I love you. For a while, My dear son, as I deal with men in divine discipline, I am often esteemed cruel and even unloving by those who really do not know what love is— oftentimes, discipline is mistaken for punishment. The true differ-

ence between discipline and punishment is the goal that I seek in applying it. I only discipline My children for their good—so that they may partake and understand the divine nature.

Do you not realize, My son that you are the temple, the place where My Holy Spirit dwells? You are My personal dwelling house. I have come to you and have shown Myself to you because you trusted and believed Me even from the beginning. I knew that you would believe Me and would follow Me, even when you had many questions and did not understand Me or believe everything I said in the beginning. However, believe Me now, the Lord your God, and trust what I said to you: 'obedience will bring forth understanding.' There are things that I will tell you that will be too great for you to understand in the beginning or formative stages of our relationship, but as you grow to know Me and the way I do things, you will never question My motive and you will understand clearly, that I am good.

My hand is upon you, My son, and My watchful gaze rests upon you when you go out and when you come in as well. I have plans for you, yes, even though you may feel that you are growing older and My ability to use you is limited. But this is what I say to you, I see you as a freshly planted tree that will bring forth much fruit—and how do I know this? Because I, the Lord, yes, I have pruned you sorely for many years, causing all the defects in you to be destroyed by My own hand. I am not saying that you are perfect in your flesh, My son, but you have been groomed so that you are wise and discerning in many areas, even in those where you have no formal training or insight. I have given you power and influence over men—not to control them, My son, but to bring them to Me, the Lord your Father and God, by giving and presenting to them the words that lead them to eternal life. Who knows where a man is on this journey in life except the Lord? Who can tell where a man is headed without failure? Only the Lord. So I look for men, those who can be trusted to honor and obey Me, and I pick them out from many and I put My signature of approval upon them and send them forth with My message. While I realize that you have had years of trouble, suffering, being doubted, rejected, and often cast aside because you were not understood, even by your peers: My plans have not failed to find their way within your heart. So now what you are doing in ministry, My son, although through much turmoil, fighting, and spiritual chaos, is exactly what I intended you to do from the very beginning—even before you heard Me say one thing about ministry to you. I am leading you; of this you can be completely sure. You can be certain that My hand is upon you and that you are not lost and never will be. Do not pay any attention to what man has to say, My son, unless it is worthy of respect and to be listened to. For My will has been deeply rooted within you through much trouble, suffering and turmoil, so that you may walk with Me and not look to the left or right or behind you. Your face should be like a solid stone, only looking forward to do the will of the One Who has called you and anointed you for such a time as this.

My son, have I not been with you all these years? Just as it was spoken by Moses to the children of Israel in the wilderness. I realize that the wilderness is not an ideal place, but it is necessary that men go through training and the process that the wilderness affords that shows and reveals to them personally what is in their hearts regarding Me, the Lord. For whatever a man says when he is suffering after many days, is truly what lives within his heart; however, after coming to his senses and seeing Me as I am through worship, the truth of Who I am and whether or not he will follow after Me, is revealed to him in his own mind. So I know what I am doing, My son, and while some often forget that I gave My Son first for the redemption and restoration of mankind, I did not take this lightly, and neither would any other man who gives his own flesh and blood whom he loves. So know this—know this from Me, the Lord God, your Father—hear Me with your whole heart when I tell you this. Abraham believed Me and he was called My very own friend—he was called My very own friend because of his faith in My words. In this day and time, My son, through Jesus Christ, My (Son), the first born from among the dead, I now call you a son because you have believed Him as He has revealed Himself and Myself. You have seen Me as I am through the representation of Jesus Christ. And His heart and desires now burn and are alive within your human spirit that you (and all those who are genuinely born again) might reveal Me, even as Jesus revealed Myself to men.

However, My dear son, I cannot be revealed through those who do not know Me, through those who have not met Me personally. I can be talked about, argued about, but in truth, only those who have met Me, who have genuinely been born again and have sat with Me can reveal and show Who I am. I am revealed My son, not discovered—I come out into the open—into public view to those who genuinely seek Me, desire and want Me, so I am not hiding. It was and continues to be a great sacrifice that Jesus has rendered, even so that you may write down these words of Mine that are given to you through the fellowship you have with Me, the Son, and the Holy Spirit. We all work together in agreement, My son, so know that your time with Me in doing My will has not ended, but you have been propelled upward through your obedience and desire to obey."

25

RETURN TO ME WITH YOUR WHOLE HEART

"I am calling you," the Lord said to the young man, "not your family. You must choose to follow Me and I will take care of what you do not understand. At this point in your life, My son, you do not know Who I am—not the way that you should. I am a responsible Father, a responsible parent, and I will teach you Who I am and I will cause you to know My way of doing things. I did not send My very own Son into the world to collectively save families all at once—not the way that you may think, but to bring a dividing sword, to separate members of families, friends, relatives, associates, so that I may deal with the hearts of those I choose individually. I call men to Myself individually and reveal Myself to men individually, sharing with them Who I am and Who they are as My very own children. This will oftentimes create confusion in the hearts of those who believe they know Me, but in reality, they have never met Me in the way that I really am.

You cannot explain what you do not know, My son, and I know that you are grieved because your family does not understand what I am doing in your life at this moment—but neither do you. However, if you will obey and follow Me, those things that you do not understand, I will make clear to you so that you will be able to follow Me and not be depressed and discouraged by the negative words and wills of family and friends. Surely, those who are called by Me, the Lord, I divinely separate and call them to Myself, so that they may grow to know the Lord, their Father, Lord and Savior, and then pursue Me for the rest of their lives in this earth and honor Me with their lives.

> "...Do not think that I have come to bring peace upon the earth; I have not come to bring peace, but a sword. For I have come to part asunder a man from his father, and a daughter from her mother, and a newly married wife from her mother-in-law— and a man's foes will be they of his own household. He who loves [and takes more pleasure in] a father or mother more than [in] Me is not worthy of Me; and he who loves [and takes more pleasure in] a son or daughter more than [in] Me is not worthy of Me." MATTHEW 10:34, 35, 36, 37

> "...Now [in Haran] the Lord said to Abram, Go for yourself [for your own advantage] away from your country, from your relatives and your father's house to the land that I will show you." GENESIS 12:1

"I am separating you from your family (for a short while) so that I may deal with you personally, so that you may know Me well. I am the Lord. For the time being you are sad because you feel that what you have worked for and labored for all these years is lost; however, that is not true. I will use you where you are, My son, and I will give back your life to you. For you do not understand altogether at this point in your life that what you have been doing is existing and not living. I have come—I have literally and actually come out into public view...I have come out into the open, even into the world, that those who receive and accept Me, the Lord, will have eternal, everlasting life. You are sad because you are leaving your family by My command. For I, the Lord, yes, I understand what it means to leave loved ones behind, but I will restore all that you think you have lost later when you realize who you are in Me as a result of being born into My kingdom, and when you know this truth from Me and the issue is settled, you will no longer be swayed in what you believe about Me or who you are as a result of Me. Then you will be able to go forward unchallenged by the opinions of others, family, friends, associates, and be led by My Holy Spirit."

"...And a crowd was sitting around Him, and they said to Him, Your mother and Your brothers and Your sisters are outside asking for You. And He replied, Who are My mother and my brothers? And looking around on those who sat in a circle about Him, He said, See! Here are my mother and My brothers; For whoever loves the things God wills is My brother and sister and mother!" MARK 3:32, 33, 34, 35

"My son, I know that for a moment you are sad, but if you will follow Me and allow Me, the Lord your God to share the truth with you about who I see you as and who you were created to be, then you will have great joy. Remember this and listen well to Me, the Lord said, if you honor Me by leaving and moving forward, I will cause your family to believe you. They will know from what I do and as a result of My intervention and treatment of you, that there has to be a God. I am He. My way of doing things is different from the way that you will do them. You can only accomplish one thing at a time, but I am busy doing many things all at once—now and for eternity. Rest now and believe Me. I will teach you and give you wisdom for how to share with your family, friends, and relatives how I, the Lord, am requiring your life at this moment. But do not expect them to altogether understand what I am saying any more than you do at this moment, for a baby cannot understand adult language; but he gradually learns adult speech in time after communication is made on his personal level. As I have told you, I am the Divine Parent, your Father and God and I have empathy for you. I know that you feel lost, but I am here to lead you and guide you, to teach you My way so that the sorrow you now feel will soon be a thing of the past. So now, do as I instruct. Place your full confidence in Me, remain with Me, listen to Me, hear My heart, and know and receive My thoughts and plans, and I will soon show you that I am your Satisfier. I will show you the way that you are to go and how you are to get there. You will have My divine assistance, and I will also teach you about times and seasons and how I bring things into your life at the appointed and perfect time. Then you will have no fear or doubt that I am fair to you and that I do not withhold good things from My children. Yes, your family will miss you and will grieve as if you are dead, for in reality, My son, you are dead to what you used to be. But even as I rose and came forth from the grave, My hand rests upon you now as one alive!"

"...And afterward I will pour out My Spirit upon all flesh; and your sons and your daughters shall prophesy, your old men shall dream dreams, your young men shall see visions." JOEL 2:28

"For this is not an entirely new thing that I am doing, for it is an old thing, a common thing that I do in My people—even those who are considered unsaved. I do a new and fresh thing in them. If you, My people, those who are called by My Name would continually honor Me and revere Me in the sanctuary, then My Presence would be more prominent and I would be able to reveal and to share My heart more openly with you.

For this is what God says: the days ahead of you are glorious—that is, if you will turn to and return to Me with your whole heart, exercising godliness through first loving each other and cultivating love where it has been lost. Then you will see a restoration of spiritual endowments among yourselves, and I, the Lord, yes, I will send teachers and instructors after My own heart. They will speak to you and encourage you in My very own nature, giving you My words and not repeating only what they have learned from men. For these that I send will be men who have actually been with Me, sitting with Me for years, learning and absorbing My ways. They shall come from among your sons and daughters and if you are not careful, you will fight with and against them, causing them to be grieved beyond measure, for they will not be able to resist My Spirit the way many have.

For this is a divinely appointed thing that I am doing, with those who rejected Me and My gifts for many years, and now, I am moving among them, bringing them into the light of My Spirit and Presence and showing Myself to them clearly. I am developing a divine hunger in them and giving them a divine strategy to take the cities and to restore the power of My Kingdom. For many of you have preached words but have lacked power behind those words. For I, the Lord, I am the only One Who can qualify and then send forth My messengers, and I am preparing them even now. Let those who listen for the Spirit's words with spiritual ears, hear what I am now speaking and sharing with My people."

SUMMARY

"... The sheep that are My own hear and are listening to My voice; and I know them, and they follow Me. And I give them eternal life, and they shall never lose it or perish throughout the ages. [To all eternity they shall never by any means be destroyed.] And no one is able to snatch them out of My hand."
JOHN 10:27, 28

It is very important that we begin to walk as the persons our heavenly Father has created and intended us to be. For many of us in the Body of Christ, it is very difficult for us to wrap our minds around the truth that we are God's sons. Although we are not perfect in the flesh, we should not allow our minds to remain wrapped around what is not perfect in us but what is now perfect in Him. The Lord has given us righteousness through Himself—righteousness that we could not obtain on our own in any way. However, we must begin to relate to that righteousness when we speak to our Father so that His face is unveiled to our spirits. So we recognize Him as the Father and the Spirit Who is now in our hearts crying "ABBA" and leading us all the more graciously into intimacy with Him.

If we are estranged from our heavenly Father, dear friends, I believe it is because we do not surrender or yield ourselves to Him as we ought. He is indeed our Father and is calling out to us as He always has, that we might come and partake of and enjoy the divine nature.

We are told this by Jesus:

"No one is able to come to Me unless the Father Who sent Me attracts and draws him and gives him the desire to come to Me, and [then] I will raise him up [from the dead] at the last day."
JOHN 6:44

This is true, we have already been drawn out of deep darkness by the Spirit of our God and He has indeed brought us into fellowship with Himself, His Son, and His Holy Spirit, and this is what He is now saying:

"Come to Me with your whole, yes your entire heart and I will reveal My whole and entire heart as it applies to your relationship with Me. For many, many years I have desired to have an open and honest and loving relationship with you, My Bride. Will you come to Me and allow Me, the Lord God, your Father, to express Myself wholly to you? I want to show you My glory and to reveal Myself to you, so that you may know Me as I am and not try to strain your eyes through the eyes of your soul to get a glimpse of Me. For if you will readily and willingly give your entire self to Me, the Lord, even

as I gave Myself fully and freely to you, then would you understand the fellowship that we now have together, that has been afforded by My obedience to the commands of My heavenly Father. But remember, dear ones that the commands of our Heavenly Father are not grievous—they revive and even nurture and even strengthen the soul, but you must come to Me. Come to Me, the Lord God your Savior, so that you may truly see that I am for you, waiting to reveal Myself, to share Myself with you, so that you may respond to Me in love.

For if you do not come to Me regularly on My own terms, then it is very difficult for you to know the precious and sincere love that I have always had for you. I long to show Myself loving, kind, considerate and compassionate toward you. Hear Me this day, (the Lord says) and no longer resist the call of My voice—recognize it, embrace it, own it, and allow that Name, that precious Name of Jesus, which has been given to you as Savior, to bring you completely to Myself, with nothing lacking as far as your needs, and then you will know Me, just as I intended from the beginning; and our fellowship—yes, yours and Mine will be unbroken as you begin to see Me face to face—spirit to Spirit, that I may express Myself. And as you grow to know Me as I am, you will see exactly that I am kind and what My intentions in fellowship with you, My people, have been all this time. Come to Me. Find your way to Me today as you sense My Holy Spirit drawing and leading you in the direction of where I am. And as you sense His leading, His drawing, do not resist Him. Yes, I am aware, (the Lord says) that He will draw you in a way that is unfamiliar and cannot be controlled by human hands, but He will draw you even until your mind is transformed and you realize, "This is the place I should have been all along, with my Father, being with Him, recognizing Him, and seeing Him as He truly is."

So today, as you hear Me calling you, don't resist Me. Don't fight with Me. Come to Me and I will listen to you—I will even hear your complaint and settle the issue with you. I, the Lord, will listen to the expression of your heart, just as good Fathers do, and then I will share My wisdom with you. However, if this is to be done the way that it should be done—fair to you and fair to Me, then you must be willing to let go of your misconceptions of who you believe that I am and be willing to exchange your ignorance for the truth. I am the Lord—I am of Age and I know Who I am and who you are, and yes, I have longed to show Myself to you just as I am, so that the devil, the true enemy of your soul will no longer have the power to torment you concerning the truth about Who I am and who you are to Me—for you are precious in My sight, and I long to be with you and to have you alongside Me—walking with Me and listening to Me, even as I listen to and respond to you. Come to Me today, My children—come to Me today and find the rest for your souls that have been wondering aimlessly all these years, and I will give you the rest that only I can give you that has already been made available to you in abundance through Jesus Christ your Lord."